Needlework
BLOCKING
and FINISHING

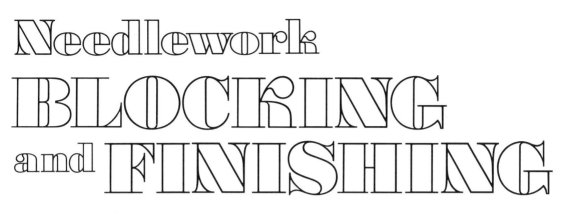

Needlework BLOCKING and FINISHING

Dorothy Burchette

Charles Scribner's Sons
New York

Library of Congress Cataloging in Publication Data

Burchette, Dorothy.
    Needlework: blocking and finishing.

    Bibliography: p.
    1. Canvas embroidery.   I. Title.
TT778.C3B87   746.4′4   73-1096
    ISBN 684-13867-0

1 3 5 7 9 11 13 15 17 19 C/MD 20 18 16 14 12 10 8 6 4 2

Printed in the United States of America

DEDICATED TO

Vivian Virginia Simpson

Acknowledgments

Many thanks to Hope Hanley, Janet Sturtevant, Betsy Edgeworth, Vivian Frisch, Bob Siebert, and Dr. Lawrence Frisch. They all know why.

Special appreciation to my husband for all the photography and my daughter Avril for her needlework and typing. Last but not least, my editor Elinor Parker certainly deserves a reward for patience.

Contents

Foreword   9

A Few Hints   11

Making the Blocking Board   13

Blocking Needlepoint   15

General Directions   23

Bathroom Seat Cover   36

Bedroom Slippers   38

Bell Pull   42

Belts   45

Covers   49

Coasters and Trivets   52

Coat Hanger   54

Cushions   56

Dog Coat   62

Brick Doorstops   64

Fly Swatter   67

Footstools   69

Glass Cases   73

Ice Bucket   75

Jewelry Roll   77

Key Chains   81

Needle Case   83
Pictures   86
Rugs   90
Sandals   97
Toe Stuffers and Pincushions   100
Wall Hangings   101
Scissors Case   103
Cosmetic Cases   105
Checkbook Cover   108
Drapery Tie-Back   110
Handbag   112
Waste Basket   115
Bibliography   125
Recommended Products   127
Needlework Sources   131
Index   133
Credits   137

Foreword

This book is designed to help you finish and mount needlework without the "home-made" look. The methods here are simplified and used successfully by professionals. It answers your question, "Now what do I do with it?"

This book is intended to show basic methods and variations. Don't hesitate to be creative and try things on your own. There are many ways to do the same thing. Hopefully, you will be inspired to try a few different projects you may have thought difficult. Materials used in the book are all readily available locally or by mail order.

The outline is in the same sequence followed to actually block and mount a piece of needlework. The methods illustrated may be used for needlepoint, crewel, all types of embroidery, including cross stitch and creative stitchery.

A Few Hints

It may seem odd to begin a book on finishing by mentioning what you should do before you start. But there are a few hints that will make blocking and finishing much easier. That "ounce of prevention", which has been around so long, is worth its weight in gold when it comes to needlework.

If, by chance, you have used water-proof markers, or something else you're not sure is run proof, to put the design on the canvas, give the painted canvas a spraying of a clear acrylic before you begin stitching. You know the acrylic is going to lock the colors in the canvas and they will not run during blocking.

DO use waterproof paints to put your design on canvas. Acrylics are good.

DO have at least two-inch unworked margins on all sides.

DO use fabric and yarns that will not run.

DO bind the edges of canvas with masking tape or turn them under and stitch them before you start. Unraveled canvas is the very devil to work with.

DO work on a frame for large pieces. It's so much faster and the needlework will need very little blocking.

DO use rust-proof pins for blocking.

Special problems arise when metallic threads are used. They should never be dampened. Synthetic threads will not tolerate steam or high temperatures, therefore, both metallic and synthetic threads should be worked on a square frame.

Do not use steam or heat when blocking silk as this will cause dry rot. Moisture may be used as mentioned later on.

Odd-shaped pieces should be blocked as if they were square. Don't cut them out of the canvas or fabric until after they are blocked.

When blocking is complete, spray with several light coats of a soil resistant product. Spray again when mounting is complete. A word of caution: these sprays can lift the most water-proof paints through the yarn. Make sure you spray just enough on the needlework to protect and not penetrate.

Making the Blocking Board

Such hard surfaces as wood, masonite, or plaster board are very difficult to work with. The easiest thing to use for blocking is insulating wall board. It is called white board in the trade as one side is sized with white paint. Pins can be inserted and removed easily. You can buy this from lumber dealers, building suppliers or some hardware stores. The sheets come four by eight feet and unless you are doing something very large, say a rug or upholstery, it is much less expensive to use a bulletin board. I find the cork bulletin boards excellent. They are a sheet of insulation board covered with a thin layer of cork and framed. They present no storage problem even in an efficiency apartment and they serve a useful purpose when not employed for blocking.

Insulation board, as it comes, or the bulletin board will have to be treated for three reasons: 1. So none of the finish can bleed onto your needlework; 2. So the board won't absorb moisture and draw colors to the right side of the needlework; 3. If the paints aren't waterproof, they will stain the board and come off onto the next piece you block.

The advantage of using the cork bulletin board is that the back is the painted side. Since this doesn't show when not used for blocking, you are free to mark it off into the one or two-inch squares for guidelines. Use a laundry-marking pen and then coat it with a clear acrylic. Of course you can use varnish or shellac, but they take longer to dry. After the acrylic is dry, dampen a paper towel or tissue and rub over the lines. If any ink comes off onto the towel, give it another coat.

If you use an ordinary bulletin board, use the back too. In this case the back is unfinished so staple white blotting paper to the back and draw your lines on this, then give it a coat of acrylic.

A one-foot square board is very useful for blocking small pieces or they can also be done on an ironing board if the padding is thick enough to pin straight down into.

See photo 1. A recent development for blocking is the "Meyer Needlepoint Blocking Device". It is reminiscent of the old curtain stretchers with pins. However, the similarity stops there. The device is engineered so you can block the most difficult and out-of-shape piece simply and by yourself. There are cranks for you to adjust in any direction and since the needlework is not against another surface it dries very quickly without the danger of mildew, etc.

1

Blocking

NEEDLEPOINT

Just about every piece of needlepoint that hasn't been worked on a frame must be blocked. If you have used a frame, a little steaming fluffs and smooths the surface which gives it a better appearance.

Do not submerge the needlepoint in water unless absolutely necessary. Sometimes the piece is so soiled it must be washed or dry cleaned. When needlepoint is washed, you remove the sizing from the canvas which was put there for two reasons:
1. To keep the threads aligned properly while you are working.
2. To keep the canvas in shape after it is worked and blocked.

Dampening the needlework and surrounding canvas loosens the sizing. It then dries and resets the threads. Washing only defeats these purposes.

It can be dry cleaned. This does not remove as much of the sizing. Be sure to use new, cleaning fluid or make sure your dry cleaning man will see to this for you. Tell him not to press it.

No amount of sizing applied to the wool after it is blocked will keep it in shape if the tension is too tight. If your piece of needlepoint has a tendency to creep on the bias after it has been blocked a few times, it will always do this because of improper tension or the stitches used. The best thing to do with it is to mount it so all edges will be fastened securely.

If pins aren't close enough together when blocking, the edges will have a reverse scallop. These out-of-line threads will show in the finished piece. Have pins about three-quarters of an inch apart or one-half inch on small pieces. Use stainless steel pins. Fortunately wig pins are stainless and available in any drug store now. T-Pins for blocking may be purchased at most knit shops. Staples will cut through canvas threads and they rust; don't use them for blocking.

I prefer to block needlepoint right side up; however, if there is any doubt at all about whether or not the paints used for the design are waterproof, it is safer to block it right side down. When needlepoint is wet, the wool acts as a wick and brings color to the surface. You want the bleeding dyes, if any, on the back of the canvas rather than the front.

If the edges of the canvas really look dangerously unraveled, as though it's going to fray when it is pinned down, turn under a narrow edge and machine stitch, zig-zag or straight stitch. If you don't have a machine, over-cast the edges. You can also apply a fabric glue to the edges. Try to have at least two inches of unworked canvas on all sides.

There is a method for salvaging a piece. If the needlepoint has been worked to within a few rows of the cut edge of canvas apply a latex glue to all edges of the needlework and allow to dry. Sew strips of a close weave (poplin, muslin etc.) fabric to the edges. For the first line of stitching have fabric and needlepoint, right sides together, and meeting at the edges. Machine stitch close to needlepoint. Fold strip flat and top stitch right next to this fold. Continue with all four sides. *See photo 68.*

When the needlepoint is not out of shape, block it dry. If there is a selvedge on one edge this must always be cut at one or two-inch intervals or cut it off if space allows. *See photo 2.* Put stainless steel pins down one side about 1″ to ¾″ apart, stretching as you pin. Line up the top or bottom of canvas with the lines on your board and pin. Continue all the way around. Simply steam with a portable steamer. That's all there is to it.

To block small pieces on an ironing board, put your needlepoint on your board right side down. *See photo 3.* Pin one corner and using a triangle, line up one side of the canvas until it's even with the edge of the triangle. Pin the other edge of the canvas even with the triangle. Move your triangle to the next corner, line it up with the straight side you already have pinned and square up the next corner. Continue all around.

Dip a clean pressing cloth, that has never been bleached, in water and wring it out. Set the iron temperature

2

3

to wool. Cover your needlepoint with the press cloth. Iron with a lifting up and down motion. *See photo 4.* Do not let the weight of the iron rest on the needlework at anytime. Lift the press cloth up immediately. If you have too much steam in the piece, or you want it to dry in a hurry, use a pounding block to pound out steam. *See photo 5.* A pounding block can be made by covering a brick with a piece of muslin. Hit it rather hard with the wide edge, straight up and down. Allow to dry on the board, then finish as required.

When small pieces of needlepoint are badly out-of-shape, cut the selvedges, if there are any. Straighten and pin one edge on the guide-line on the board. Line up and pin the top edge next. Start pinning the bottom edge. You will find this rather difficult; ripples begin to form. *See photo 6.* Apply steam with a portable steamer the full length of the canvas (top to bottom) and pull as you steam. If pulling is difficult use canvas pliers. Insert a pin when the edge you are pulling is on a straight line. Continue across the bottom and then do the final side. You will have to give it plenty of steam to make the canvas and yarn give enough to straighten the edge. When it is pinned on every side, spray all stitching

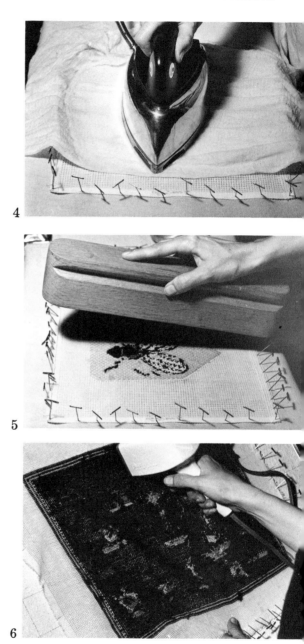

4

5

6

and surplus canvas with a very fine mist but don't wet it too much. *See photo 7*. You want it thoroughly damp, not wet. Leave the damp canvas on the blocking board for at least 24 hours after it is dry.

Very large pieces that are badly out of shape require what is called "London Shrink". Keep a special cloth that has not been washed in bleach for blocking. It should be at least six inches wider and one foot longer than the piece to be dampened. An old sheet is good.

Wet the cloth completely and wring out, not too dry. Lay it on a flat surface and put the needlepoint on over it, placed near the top. Fold the surplus fabric over the bottom and continue folding both pieces together. Cover this with another piece of wet cloth and leave it for two to three hours or until the wool and canvas are both very moist. If you think they will dry too quickly, cover with a piece of plastic. Kitchen plastic wrap or an old dry-cleaning bag are good. Unwrap and pin the needlework to a sheet of insula-

7

tion board immediately. Here again, leave on at least 24 hours after it is dry.

Always let all needlepoint dry where there is plenty of ventilation and light, but not in the sun or near a source of high heat. Mold and mildew can form in just a few hours, especially in humid weather.

CREWEL

Crewel should always be washed if it has been worked in a round hoop.

You don't have to turn the edges under or stitch them unless the background fabric is very loosely woven.

To wash crewel, mix a mild solution of "Woolite", or similar product, and warm water in a bowl large enough to submerge the embroidery. Put in the crewel and agitate it for a few seconds. Do not allow it to soak as you're only inviting the colors to run. Lift it out and drain briefly, then rinse at least three times in clean water the same temperature. Have a thick turkish towel ready, lay the needlework on the towel and roll it up. Gently press the roll with your hands so the towel absorbs excess moisture. If it is still wet, repeat the rolling and gentle pressing in a clean, dry towel. If the wool has run, rinse, rinse and rinse some

more. Do not let it dry like this. Treat it for stain removal before it dries (See page 116.)

Lay the embroidery on the blocking board face up so the stitches will be raised and not flattened.

Put the first pin in the center of the top edge of the fabric. Pull the fabric at the bottom opposite the first pin and insert the next pin in the center of the bottom edge. *See photo 8.* Put the third pin in the center edge of the right side of the fabric. Be sure you don't pull the center threads, running from top to bottom, out of alignment. They should be straight up and down. Put the fourth pin in the center of the edge of the left side. Here again, be sure not to pull the threads of the background fabric out of alignment. Place the next pins on either side of the first pin (top), then on either side of the second pin (bottom); then the sides. Stretch the fabric before you pin. Continue pinning on opposite sides first top, then bottom, then right side and left side until all sides are pinned every half inch. Pull as you go, to keep the background fabric smooth. *See photo 9.* When all sides have pins about one-half inch apart, let it dry in a light and well-ventilated area, but not in the direct sunlight or near a source of heat.

8

9

Round cushions and rugs are easier to block on an insulation-board template cut to the exact finished measurement of the article. Dampen by the "London" method and turn seam allowance over the edge of the template and pin in place. Let dry thoroughly. You now have a crease as a guide line for stitching or turning over. *See photo 10.*

SILK EMBROIDERY

Put a piece of white blotter between the blocking board and the silk to allow it to dry quicker. Pin out and spray a fine mist over entire back of the embroidery. Water stains silk if it is not moistened evenly. There must be *no* dry spots, but avoid getting it too wet. Allow to dry on the board.

10

General Directions

INVISIBLE THREAD

Invisible nylon mono-filament thread is always used. Thread your needle with double the amount needed plus 1 foot extra. Fold it over in your needle and knot the ends with a figure-eight knot:

1. Hold ends of thread between thumb and index finger of right hand. Other end is held with little and ring fingers of the same hand. Put index finger of left hand through loop, from the back.

2, 3, & 4. shows one complete turn towards you with the left hand. Palm of left hand should be facing you when turn is complete.

5. Pass the ends through the loop you have just made, from the back, with the thumb and index finger of the right hand.

6. Knot will look like a figure 8. Pull the knot tight and clip the loose ends to ¼″.

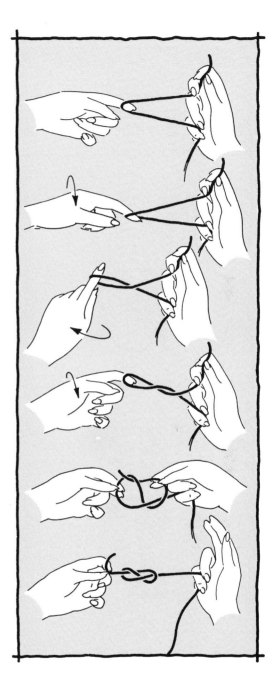

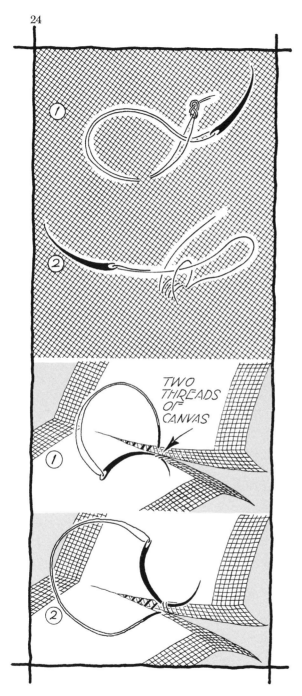

TWO
THREADS
OF
CANVAS

First Stitch

1. Take a small stitch through the fabric. Do not pull thread tight. Pass the needle between the two threads below the knot. Now pull the thread tight.

Last Stitches

2. Take five small stitches very close together. Pull them tight. Take one more stitch and before pulling it tight, pass the needle under this last stitch. Now pull tight.

BLIND STITCH

You must use a curved needle and work from the right side. Fold edges of fabric under and lay both folds of fabric together so they just meet. Pin to a firm surface (blocking or ironing board) at both ends of seam.

1. Pick up two threads of canvas on one folded edge. Make sure you catch canvas and not design threads.

2. Pick up two threads of canvas on the other folded edge, exactly opposite the point where your needle came out of the last stitch. Continue alternating to end.

This is the only professional meth-

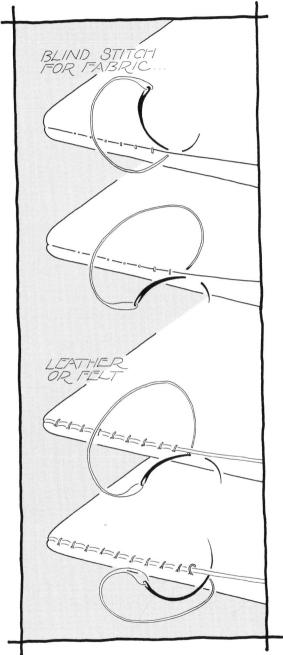

BLIND STITCH
FOR FABRIC...

LEATHER
OR FELT

od for hand-joining fabrics. Once you acquire the knack of using invisible thread and a small curved needle you will find the results well worth the effort.

Fold and pin seam allowances under. Anchor the article to a firm surface with pins so you will have both hands free to control the thread. Work on the right side of the fabric exactly on the seam line. Stitches may be from $\frac{1}{8}$″ to $\frac{1}{2}$″ long depending on weight of fabric, size of article, etc.

Fabric to Fabric

1. Thread is anchored within seam allowance. First stitch extends under several threads on the top fold. Pull thread through fabric.
2. Make your next stitch the same size on the opposite fold of fabric directly below the end of the last stitch. Continue alternating from one fold to the other.

Leather to Fabric

Sometimes leather, "Ultrasuede," felt, etc., require a clean-cut edge (without folded seam allowances). Anchor thread within seam allowance of fabric. Stitches are ⅛″ in from cut edge of leather.

1. Push needle from wrong side of leather through to right side. Bring thread over cut edge of leather.

2. Next stitch is under several threads of fold on the opposite seam line. As the needle emerges from this stitch push it through the leather from the wrong side. Continue alternating leather to fold to end of seam.

MITERED CORNERS

Corners are mitered on the back of the needlework.

1. Surplus fabric or canvas edges beyond design area are measured and cut to the same width.

2. Corners must be true. You can mark the fold line on the right side. Use tailor's chalk.

3. Bring point of corners towards center of design.

4. Press the folded edge to keep it in place.

5. Fold top straight edge over towards center.

6. "T" pin it in place to ironing or blocking board and press edge.

7. Fold and press side edge the same way.

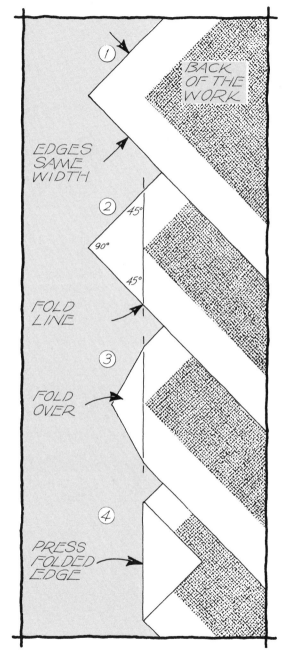

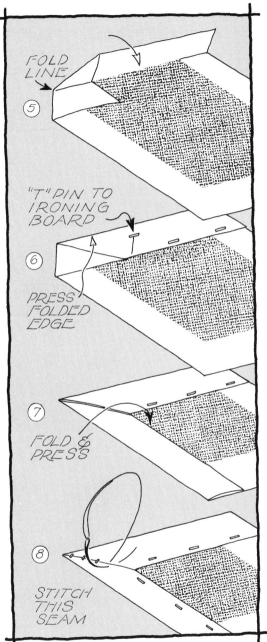

FOLD LINE

⑤

"T" PIN TO IRONING BOARD

⑥

PRESS FOLDED EDGE

⑦

FOLD & PRESS

⑧

STITCH THIS SEAM

8. Hand sew the diagonal seam at the corner.

To miter four corners, press the points in place first, then do the sides.

BIAS CORDING

Cutting Bias Strips

1. Fabric sides and ends must be straight and corners squared.
2. Bring bottom edge over to meet side.
3. Press this diagonal line.
4. Open fabric and place a clear plastic (C-thru) ruler along the pressed fold line. Use a chalk dressmaker's pencil to draw a line, the full length, one inch from the fold.
5. Continue to draw lines one inch apart until you have as many strips as you need. Cut strips apart on these lines.

Stitching

1. Have right sides of fabric together with points overlapping at edge. Start stitching at point shown. Sew as many strips together as you need to give you one continuous piece as long as required.
2. Press all seams open on the wrong

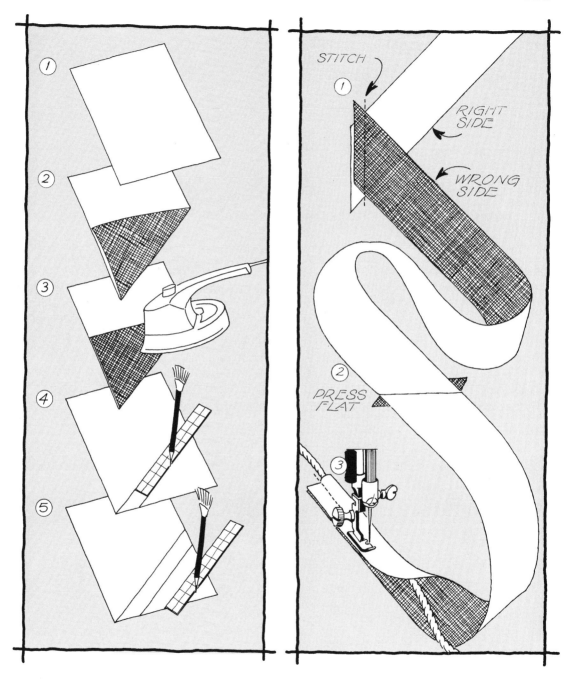

side. You can cut off the points that extend beyond the edge if you like but it isn't necessary.

3. Attach zipper foot to your machine and adjust the stitch to a long length. Fold the bias fabric with right side out, over purchased cotton cord and machine stitch close to the cord.

Square Corners-Starting and Stopping

11

Start sewing at the lower right or left corner of the needlework design. Right side of needlework should be uppermost and raw edges of cording and needlework together. Stitch completely around needlework.

See photo 11. When you have stitched almost to the last inch of the cording, push the bias back to expose the cotton cord inside. Cut this last ¾″ off. *See photo 12.* Continue stitching the empty bias across the end.

12

Curved Edge-Starting and Stopping

See photo 13. Begin applying bias cording with the end running off the edge of the canvas at an angle. Stitch around needlework until you reach the last inch. Push the bias back to expose the cotton cord. Cut the last ¾″ off.

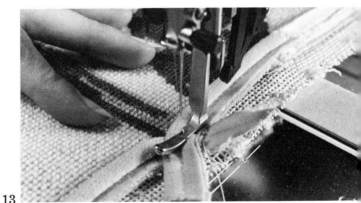

13

FOLD FABRIC OVER PLASTIC RULER & PRESS

Lap the empty bias over the other end. As you stitch over the two ends of bias, pull the last end over the edge at an angle.

Sewing Around Corners

Cording must be clipped at the corners as it is applied.

1. *Square Corner.* Stitch to the turning point at the corner. Leave the machine needle in the fabric. Clip the bias only to the stitching line. Turn the fabric and continue stitching down the straight edge.

2. *Round corner or edge.* Stitch on curve and clip as outer edge of bias begins to turn up (about every one or two inches depending on curve).

Flat Bias Band

Cut bias strips according to directions on page 27. Sew together as shown on page 28. A 1″ finished band would be made of strips 2″ wide or cut the strip two times the desired finished width.

1. *First side.* Fold ½″ of fabric to the wrong side over a clear plastic (C-thru) ruler. Steam press as you fold. Continue down full length of strip.

2. *Second side.* Fold other edge ½″ over the clear plastic ruler and.press as you fold the full length.

Back of Cushion

Put the zipper foot on machine to sew the fabric over the bias cording. Cut fabric backing the same size as the front of cushion. Lay the fabric over the needlework, right sides together. *See photo 14.* Begin stitching about 2″ from the corner. Continue around cushion to 2″ past the fourth corner. This leaves the bottom partially open for turning.

14

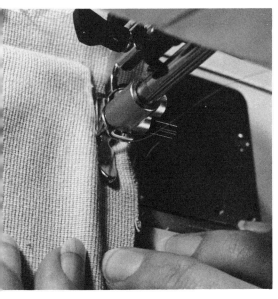

BINDING STITCH

This is the needlework application 15

of the centuries old "Round Braid" stitch used to bind and join leather. As in leather work the hole count can be varied and it can also be worked on flat canvas as a decorative line stitch.

It is worked over two threads on edge of canvas for binding a single piece. To join two pieces of canvas work over one thread from each piece of canvas. Needle is always inserted through canvas from back to front.

1. To start, push needle from back to front through first hole. Hold a short end of thread in the back to be covered as you proceed.

2. *See photo 15.* Push needle from back to front through second hole,

then through first hole again. This forms a cross stitch over the edge.

3. *See photo 16.* Push needle from back to front through third hole.

4. *See photo 17.* Push needle from back to front through second hole.

5. *See photo 18.* Push needle from back to front through fourth hole.

Continue forward two holes and back one.

Run your needle back under several stitches to end the row.

Variations

A thicker edge can be worked by changing the count to forward 3, 4 or 5 and back 2, 3 or 4.

17

16

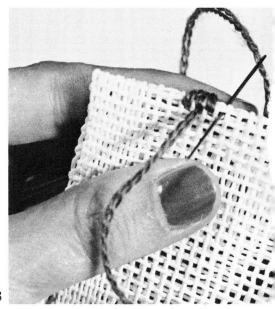

18

TWISTED CORD

This type of cord can be made any length and is used around edges of cushions. You can make lengths a little longer than each edge of the cushion and knot them together at the corners for self tassels or make one length to fit completely around the cushion. Blind stitch to the edge. A single length, knotted at both ends, can be used for wall hangings.

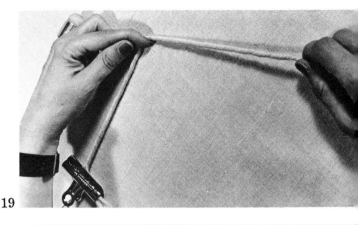

See photo 19. Secure several strands of yarn to any stationary object and twist strands rather tight. Place your finger in the center of the length and bring one end back to the other end. *See photo 20.* When you remove your finger the cord twists back on itself. Knot the loose end. Roll it on a flat surface with the palm of your hand to make it smooth and evenly twisted. Use as desired.

TOOLS—(TOP TO BOTTOM)

See photo 21. 1. Artist's canvas pliers: Used for stretching heavier, larger pieces and canvas with very tight tension. The protrusion on the lower bar serves as a fulcrum to give you greater leverage.

2. Linoleum printing roller. Used to smooth and exert even pressure when

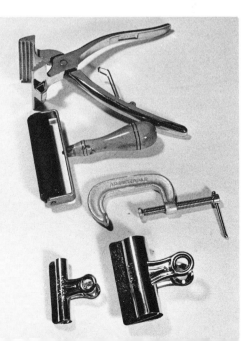

two pieces are glued together and a close bond is required.

3. C-clamp: Used to exert pressure in small areas and with pressure boards.

4. "Bulldog" clips: Used to hold corners etc. temporarily while being glued.

APPLYING PRESSURE

See photo 22. Two boards, sanded smooth, are used to apply great pressure to books, belts, etc. The boards should be a few inches larger on all sides than whatever you intend to glue. These boards happen to be 6″ x 12″ x ½″. Belts are glued a section at a time.

Cover the top and bottom of whatever you are going to glue with waxed paper. Put the object between the boards and clamp them together with C-clamps tight as possible.

NEEDLEWORK SIZING

Basic Formula: Mix 7 T. cold water with 1 T. rice flour. Bring to boil. Brush on back of needlepoint while still hot.

Medium Formula: 6 T. water to 1 T. rice flour.

Heavy Formula: 5 T. water to 1 T. rice flour.

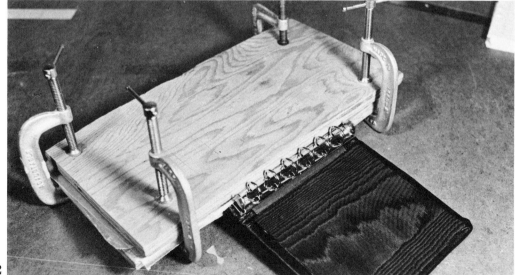

22

Crewel Embroidery and Paste: Dilute basic formula with an equal amount of boiling water.

Store unused portion in refrigerator up to 1 week. Heat for re-use.

I have experimented with many, many materials for sizing. Rice flour seems to work better than anything else. It does not damage needlework. Bugs are not attracted to it nor does it mold after it is dry or have an objectionable odor.

HELPFUL ODDS AND ENDS

1. Begin machine stitching parallel edges at the same end for each edge. Otherwise, there is just enough pull from the pressure foot to make edges creep in opposite directions and the needlework is pulled off-grain. It will never hang straight or lie flat.

2. When hand sewing seams, etc., pin the article to your ironing board and raise it to almost eye-level. This relieves strain and leaves both hands free for controlling the thread. Have the ironing board well padded so you can pin straight down into it.

3. You won't loose any of the design area for seams if you work two extra rows of needlepoint around the edge of cushions or anything that is to be machine seamed.

4. It is very difficult to cut small round holes in needlepoint for inserting eyelets or snaps. Use a die punch (which must be hit with a hammer) instead of the pliers type punch. Die punches are available in different sizes to fit all size snaps etc.

5. Let invisible thread run through your fingers when winding the bobbin or wind it by hand. Wind slowly and loosen the tension on the bobbin case slightly before stitching. The monofilament has a high degree of elasticity. If it is wound too tight on the bobbin it creates a bind, causing uneven stitches and thread breakage.

Bathroom Seat Cover

Block needlepoint as required. Measure the distance across the base between the bolts that hold the seat in place on the commode. Add 2″ to this measurement. Cut a 2″ bias strip this length. Measure from bolt to bolt around the outer long edge of needle-point. Add 2″ to this measurement. Cut another 2″ bias strip this length.

Trim needlepoint canvas away. Apply latex glue to this cut edge to prevent raveling. *See photo 23.* Turn back the ends of the long bias strips and sew in place, right sides together.

Turn back ends of short bias strip and sew this in place. Trim all seams to ¼″.

Lay needlepoint on top of canvas-lining fabric and draw the outline of the needlework on the canvas. Cut this out and set it aside temporarily.

Fold the short section of bias, at the base of seat, over the edge to the back. Pin in place and machine stitch,

24

23

25

through all layers. *See photo 24.* Use the zipper foot for stitching and sew right next to the canvas bias.

Lay the lining canvas down flat. Place the needlepoint (right sides together) on top. Pin the long bias strip to the edge of the lining. *See photo 25.* Stitch this in place. (It will look like a box cushion with a large open gap at the base.) Fold back the raw edge of the lining at the opening and machine stitch close to this edge through the lining only. Turn the whole thing inside out.

26

See photo 26. Align stitched edge of bias strip on top with the stitched edge of the bias strip on the canvas lining.

Stick pins through needlework to help with this alignment. Baste in place. Machine stitch through all layers at the edge of the bias strip. Use the zipper foot. You have made a casing for the cotton cord and attached the lining in one operation. Use a bodkin to thread the cotton cord through the bias binding around the edge of the seat cover. Tie large knots in each end of the cord. *See photo 27.*

The final blocking is done right on the seat. Spray edges of needlework with water. Put the cover on the lid and tie in place.

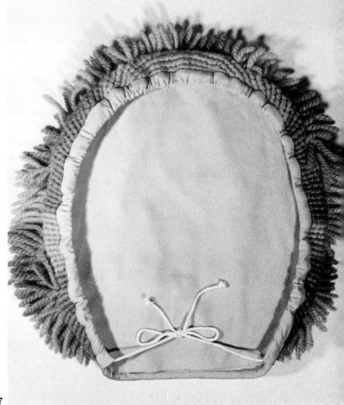

27

Bedroom Slippers

Block as required and brush a medium sizing solution to back of slippers. Ultrasuede is used for lining and top and bottom of soles. Two pairs of Dr. Scholl's Foam Insoles (large men's size) are used for interlining slipper soles. Polyester braid binds the edges.

TOP OF SLIPPERS

See photo 28. Use dressmakers tracing paper and tracing wheel to mark outline of slipper toe section on Ultrasuede. Add a ½″ seam allowance. Cut out the toe lining.

See photo 29. Block toe sections over a pair of tennis shoes. Stuff the toe of the shoe with something so they will be firm. Spray the outer edges (not the instep) and toe of the needlepoint and unworked canvas with water. Pin to the lower edge of the sole easing out fullness as you pin. You will be surprised how easy this is. Allow to dry thoroughly. Block the Ultrasuede lining the same way but use steam instead of spraying with water.

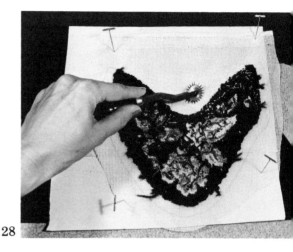

28

29

Machine stitch the lining to the needlepoint at the curved instep seam just inside the edge of the needlepoint, right sides together. *See photo 30.* Clip seam allowance every ½″ right to the needlepoint.

38

Open and turn this section to the right side. Smooth all seam allowances toward and under the lining. *See photo 31.* Top stitch, on the lining and through all seam allowances, ⅛″ from edge of needlepoint. Turn lining to underside and steam press this edge. Use a pounding block to get a nice flat, sharp edge.

30

SOLE

Put the tennis shoes on top of a pair (fabric sides out) of foam insoles. Draw the outline of the shoe on the insole with a felt-tipped pen. Cut on this line. Use a pair of insoles for each slipper. Lay the insole on the Ultrasuede and draw the outline of the insole. Add ½″ seam allowance around edge. Cut out four of these Ultrasuede linings. Make sure you cut pairs and not twins.

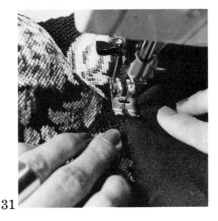

31

Trim the canvas at the base of the needlepoint heel section to ¼″. *See photo 32.* Clip canvas to needlepoint at center. Turn ¼″ seam allowance under and pin heel section to top sole lining. Machine stitch on needlepoint heel section to lining at this edge. Do not stitch completely around heel.

Pin sole linings together with foam insoles between the two pieces of Ul-

32

trasuede. *See photo 33.* Use the zipper foot to machine stitch right next to the insoles all the way around the sole.

See photo 34. It's time for a fitting. Place the sole on a blocking board. Pin fit the toe section over your foot, pinning into the blocking board. Try to pin through the seam line on the sole. Take your foot out, remove the slipper (intact) from the blocking board. *See photo 35.* Machine stitch toe section to sole along pinned line. Trim entire outer edge of sole to ¼ ″.

See photo 36. Pin one edge of woven braid over edge of sole, covering previously stitched seam line on top of slipper. Fold ends of braid under and butt ends at inner instep. Machine stitch close to edge of braid.

Fold braid over edge of slipper. Turn loose edge of braid under and pin to stitched seam line on bottom of slipper. Use invisible thread and a curved needle to blind stitch (see page 25) edge of braid to Ultrasuede sole. *See photo 37.*

33

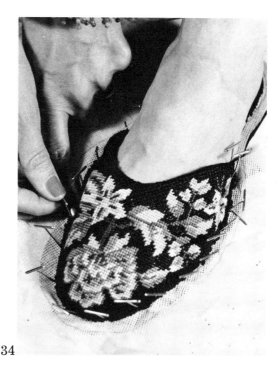

34

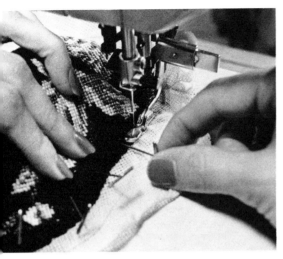

35

36

37

Bell Pull

METHOD I

Block as required. Apply sizing if needlework has a tendency to creep out of shape. (See page 34.) First trim edges of canvas about a half inch narrower than back opening of bell-pull hardware. *See photo 38*. Use invisible thread and a long stitch on your machine to sew the needlepoint to backing fabric with right sides together. Stitching should be over one row of needlepoint.

Trim seam of fabric even with canvas. The next seam must be sewn by hand. Place needlework onto padded ironing board and pin in place, right side up. *See photo 39*. Fold raw edge of velvet over canvas and turn it under on sewing line. Pin in place. Begin hand stitching at the same end machine stitching was started. (See page 25.) Using curved needle and invisible thread, blind stitch this side in place.

38

39

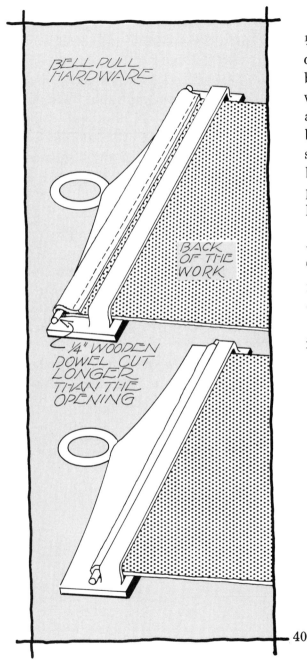

BELL PULL
HARDWARE

BACK
OF THE
WORK

1/4" WOODEN
DOWEL CUT
LONGER
THAN THE
OPENING

40

Trim top and bottom of canvas to ½″. Apply latex to edges so canvas does not unravel. *See photo 40.* Slip bell pull through hardware. Lay wooden or plastic ¼″ doweling on top and bottom ends. Fold over velvet and blind stitch in place. Leave open on sides so doweling can be removed. Pull bottom and top pieces of hardware into place. Give it a final steaming and hang. *See photo 41.*

Attaching the bell pull with dowels will facilitate its removal for cleaning. This particular bell pull was too narrow for the hardware so a wide (1″) edging was necessary. When the bell pull fits the hardware the velvet edging is not as wide so it resembles piping.

41

METHOD II

Sew the lining fabric and embroidery together with right sides out. Stitch both sides beginning at the same end. This edge is cut clean (no turn-unders) and covered with a decorative braid. The braid on top and bottom is left open at the sides for inserting and removing the dowels.

LUGGAGE RACK STRAPS

Luggage straps are finished the same as bell pulls. Of course you won't need the wooden dowels at each end. Simply clean cut the ends ½″ beyond finished portion of needlework. Fold these ends under and attach to the bottom sides of the rack with decorative upholsterer's tacks.

Belts

The preferred method of working needlepoint is to turn down three or four rows of canvas on each long edge and stitch the design through the double thickness of canvas. Leave the last row of canvas unworked for the binding stitch to be applied after the belt is blocked.

If you have not worked through the double canvas, another method is to apply latex to all edges. *See photo 42.* Fold edges to back of belt and apply pressure (see General Directions). *See photo 43.* Still another method is to fold edges over to back and secure in place with long herringbone stitches.

Ultrasuede makes an excellent lining but you may use any light to medium-weight fabric with a firm weave. Cut Ultrasuede 1″ shorter than each 10″ of belt length. A 30″ belt would have an Ultrasuede lining cut to 27″. Fasten the Ultrasuede to each end and stretch it in between. Fabric interlinings should be cut ½″ shorter than belt and the needlework eased between the ends.

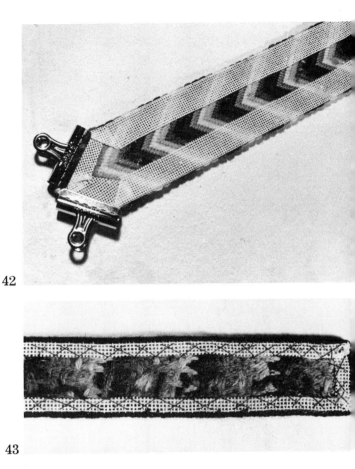

42

43

Hand blind stitching may be used to join the edges of needlework and lining together. *See photo 44.* You can also use fusing tape (Stitch Witchery or something similar) sandwiched between lining and cover. If you want to machine stitch use invisible thread and you must start sewing at the same end

45

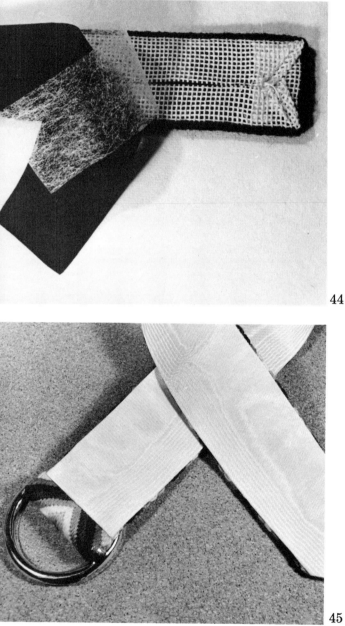

44

45

on both edges. *See photo 45.* The most professional method is to apply latex cream to the entire back of the belt, position the lining and apply pressure (see page 34).

Block by pinning one end to the tip of your ironing board, steam, pull and pin the other end. Allow to dry. Buckles with prongs are not covered all the way to the end that attaches to the buckle. Two inches of canvas are left unworked. This short end is covered with lining on the needlework side and slit where the prong is to go through the belt. Eyelets are used at the holes for the prong. Use a hole punch instead of scissors to make the opening for the eyelets. When eyelets are used a firm interlining ("Permette") is glued between lining and belt, extending ½″ beyond first and last eyelets.

Belts with center-post buckles should be made about 6″ longer than waist measurement. One inch is allowed for folding over the buckle post. Three eyelets are inserted in the other end. The center eyelet is the exact waist measurement.

Lightly steam belts when completed and allow to dry loosely rolled instead of out flat.

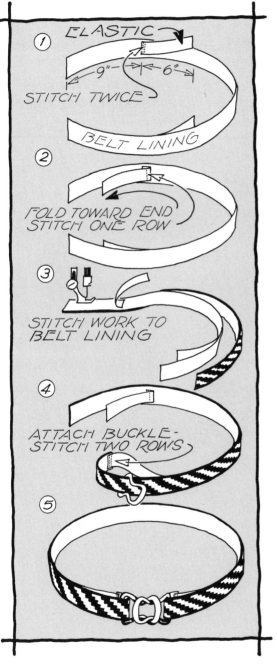

MEN'S STRETCHABLE BELT

Work needlepoint a minimum of 5″ longer than waist measurement. Stitch the design through folded-back double canvas. Work binding stitch on all edges. Cut belt lining (purchased belting was used here). Cut two 6″ lengths of non-roll elastic (same width as belt lining). 1. Attach elastic 9″ from end of lining, with two rows of machine stitching. 2. Fold elastic toward end and top-stitch next to fold with one row of stitching. 3. Use invisible thread to machine stitch lining to belt. Start at one end, stitch to elastic. Lower feed on machine and stitch in place a few times. Raise feed but do not cut thread to begin sewing on the other side of the elastic. Continue to other piece of elastic and sew this the same way. Sew both sides starting from the same end. 4. Slip the buckles over the ends and fasten elastic to needlework with two rows of stitching. 5. Completed belt stretches when necessary.

DOUBLE EYELET BELT

I had a metal sculptor make this 2-prong buckle for me so I could interchange belts with a minimum amount of effort. Different width belts simply have an eyelet in each end.

Make a belt by any of the previously described methods to your exact waist measurement. Measure distance between the two prongs of the buckle and set your eyelets one-half of this distance from each end of the belt.

Leather and suede belts are used with the buckle in addition to various needlework. *See photo 46.*

46

Book Covers

These same directions may be used to cover purchased address, appointment, telephone books or photo album. I have found the inexpensive paper-covered books to be very satisfactory. The loose-leaf type book is preferred. Do not use slick plastic books unless you want to get involved with highly toxic and flammable cements. Ultrasuede or real leather may be used for the outside cover.

LINING

Have at least ½″ to ¾″ surplus fabric or canvas around needlework.

Measure the inside of the book to the point where it folds and cut a piece of "Perma-Crin" ⅛″ smaller on all sides. Choose a light to medium weight fabric (moiré or silk, etc.) for the lining and cut it ½″ larger on all sides than this measurement. Lay the "Perma-Crin" interlining over the wrong side of the lining fabric. Apply latex cream to one edge at a time and fold the fabric edges over the interlining. (You don't have to mitre corners.) Make a front and back lining in this manner and put them under pressure while you continue. *See photo 48.*

OUTSIDE COVER

Measure the outside cover of the book and have a mat cut (or do it yourself—artist's mat board available at picture framers) to these dimensions. Mat edges must be at least ½″ wide. *See photo 47.* Measure your needlework, insert and cut the center out so

47

48

49

it will cover the last row of stitching or ¼ ″ wider on all sides than needlework design area. Cut the center section you have just removed ¼ ″ smaller than center opening. All edges on mat and center section should be beveled.

Lay the open book on your covering material and cut this at least ¾ ″ larger on all sides.

Position the mat over the covering, on the wrong side and glue in place with latex cream. Cut out the center opening leaving ½ ″ to ¾ ″ for turn under. *See photo 48.* Cut each corner diagonally right to the mat. Turn these edges under and glue in place.

Cover the center section with latex and put your needlework on this. *See photo 49.* Apply latex to all edges of surplus needlework and glue this to the back of the front cover. Finally, apply latex cream to the entire front of the book and position the cover, with the needlework insert, and put the whole front cover under pressure for at least 1 hour. After the front is firmly set, latex the back (spine too if it is wide) and apply pressure for about 10 minutes.

INSIDE LINING

Open the book, fold and glue

edges of covering to inside of book. Pull the points of the covering into position with the surplus tucked under on both sides of the point. Glue corners in place. *See photo 50.*

Spread latex over the back of the front lining before you put it in place and under pressure for about 10 minutes. Do the inside back the same way. Put a dab of latex under the folded edge over the spine and push it under the ends of the loose-leaf portion with a knife or nail file. The dark book is covered with calf; the other with Ultrasuede. *See photo 51.*

50

51

Coasters and Trivets

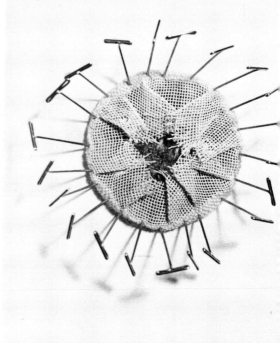

COASTERS

Coasters and trivets are made by the same method. Block the coaster by method required and apply a light coat of sizing to the back. Allow to dry.

Measure diameter of coaster. Cut an interlining of "Permette" ¼" smaller than finished size. Center the "Permette" over the coaster. Fold raw edges to back, steaming as you fold. *See photo 52*, pin in place and allow to dry. The needlepoint stitches must cover the edge of the interlining. Clip away surplus canvas.

Cut a circle of ⅛" cork slightly larger than needlework. Adhere cork to back of coaster with latex cream. Apply pressure for about 1 hour. Trim cork from edge of coaster. Spray the top with several light coats of a soil-resistant product. *See photo 53.*

TRIVETS

Trivets are mounted with a piece

of cardboard under the "Permette" for strength. One-quarter inch thick cork is used for the bottom.

GLASS TRIVET

The narrow metal frames, available in any size strips are used. Simply block and size the needlework. Cut it to fit the frame and lay it over a piece of cardboard. Cover it with a piece of Pyrex glass cut to the proper size. Insert everything into the frame and cover the back with cork.

The needlework in the trivet pictured was too small for the frame so a silk mat was made to cover the edges. *See photo 54.*

Coat Hanger

Block and size as required. Measure all the way around the needlepoint edge to find out how much cording you will need. Cut your strips for this and make cord (see page 28). Save one strip about 6″ long for tubing to cover the wire part of hanger. Fold this strip in half and seam across one end and down the side. Turn this tubing right side out and slide it over the metal portion of the hanger. *See photo 55.* Tack or glue the bottom of tubing in place.

Sew cording to right side of needlepoint with line of stitching as close to edge of needlepoint as possible. *See photo 56.* The finished edge of cording should be towards the center of the needlework. Pin backing fabric and needlepoint right sides together. Start stitching on top edge of hanger from end towards top center. Leave ½″ open at center top to insert wire part of hanger. Leave bottom open. Clip at sharp corners and turn needlework inside out.

Cut away surplus canvas and fabric leaving about ½″ seam on top

edges and ¾″ to 1″ on bottom edge. After it is turned, insert hanger through ½″ space you left open at the top.

Starting at one end, blind stitch for about 2″, anchor your thread temporarily, and use dacron batting to stuff around the wooden portion of the hanger. Continue in this manner, sewing for 2″ and stuffing. When you reach the center, fasten thread and begin working at the other end. Give it a final light steaming. *See photo 57.*

55

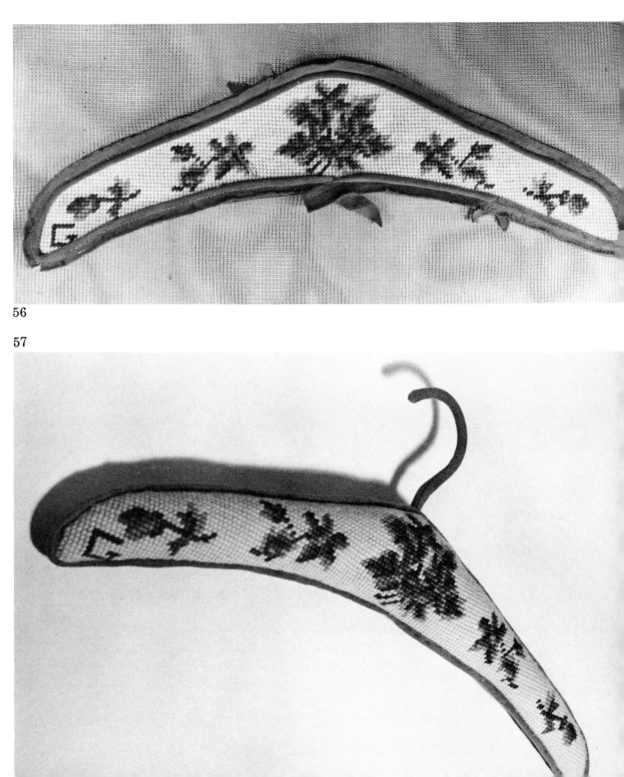

56

57

Cushions

FABRICS FOR BACK

When you make your own cushions, or bolsters, select a fabric that complements, accents, or harmonizes with colors in the needlework. Pick one similar in weight to needlepoint or embroidery. Suitable fabrics are:

Needlepoint

> Upholster's Velveteen (Med. wt.)
> Antique Silk
> Ultrasuede
> Moiré

Crewel etc.

> Linen
> Same fabric as front
> Antique Silk
> Moiré

FILLERS:

Down is the preferred filler for needlepoint and embroidery. Upholsterers will make these forms to order for you even though you are covering it yourself.

Dacron batting can be purchased in many fabric stores, drapery departments and at some upholstery shops. It is about the same as old-fashioned horsehair.

Polyfoam forms can be purchased molded to shape or in different lengths and thickness. If you have to cut it yourself use a felt-tipped pen to mark and cut with an electric carving knife or very sharp scissors. Better results are obtained if foam rubber is covered with muslin first.

EDGINGS

Cushions look better and keep a firmer edge when a trim is used. You can use bias cording, fringe, purchased cording or sew on a twisted wool cord. It is advisable to preshrink the filler cord before bias cording is made if it is to be used on a washable cushion. Any of the above may be substituted for bias cording in the following directions.

See photo 58. I have found zippers too bulky for cushions and do not use them. Sew the opening together with invisible thread and curved needle.

KNIFE-EDGE CUSHIONS

Specific instructions for every-

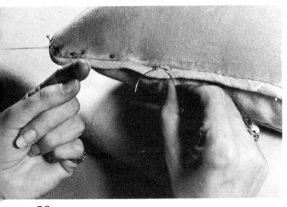

58

thing in printed italics are in chapter General Directions.

See photo 59. Block needlework as required. Make *bias cording* and *stitch it to the face of the needlework.* Cut backing fabric to size and with right sides together, *stitch backing to needlework.* Leave an opening to turn and fill. Sew opening together with *invisible thread.*

BOXED CUSHIONS

Block needlework. Make *bias cording* and stitch it to the face of the needlework. Cut the fabric back and *stitch bias cording* around the edges of this also.

Cut a straight-of-grain length of fabric the circumference of the cushion plus a seam allowance. Seam the ends

59

and join the two sections of the cover with this strip of fabric. Leave an opening on the edge of the back fabric to turn and fill. Sew opening together with invisible thread.

VARIATIONS

Knife Edge-Tucked Corner

A round corner is easier to sew than a square one. *See photo 60.* Take a ½″ tuck in each corner of the needlework on a square cushion. *See photo 61.* Fold the tuck to the back when you sew the bias cording in place. Take a ½″ tuck in the corners of the fabric for the back before you put the cushion together. *See photo 62.* End the cording along the edge of the cushion to eliminate bulk.

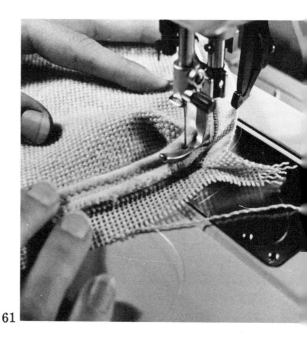

61

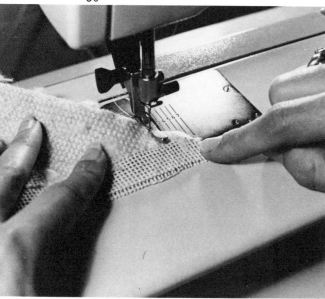

60

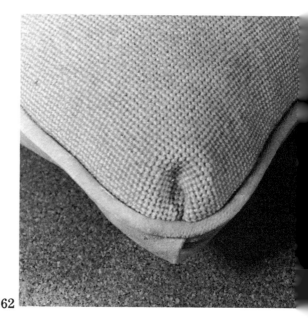

62

ROUND NEEDLEWORK, SQUARE CUSHION

Cut the front and back of cushion and make *bias cording* of the same fabric.

Make a *folded bias strip* the circumference of the needlework. Cut edges of needlework to a perfect circle. Apply latex cream to the cut edge. Position and pin the needlework in the center of the previously cut piece of fabric. *See photo 63.* Machine stitch the bias strip through all thicknesses. Fold bias strip over edge of needlework. *See photo 64.* Pin in place and hand sew this edge with invisible thread and a curved needle. *See photo 65.* Seam the ends of the bias strip last. Construct the cushion as usual. *See photo 66.*

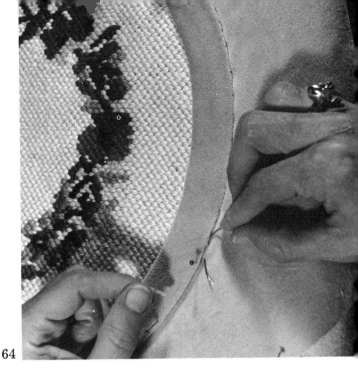

64

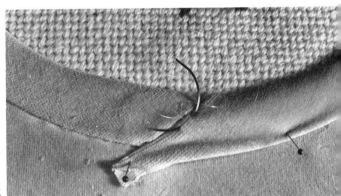

63

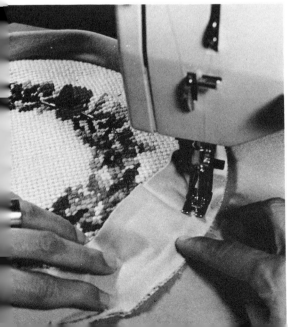

65

66

BOXED FLOOR CUSHION

See photo 67. Apply latex glue to all edges, right up to the needlepoint. Allow to dry. *See photo 68.* This canvas is so loosely woven that strips of upholsterer's canvas were sewn to all edges close to the needlepoint.

See photo 69. Pin the needlepoint to the top of the cushion. Measure face of needlework. To this measurement, add the depth of the cushion of each side plus ½″ seam allowance on all edges. This cushion measures 20″ x 20″. The polyfoam filler is 4″ thick,

so the back fabric (Ultrasuede is used here) is 29″ x 29″. *See photo 70.* Fold fabric on a diagonal. Use a triangle to mark the corner seams line at cushion depth plus ½″. Sew corner on this marked line on the inside of the fabric. Mark and sew each corner this same way.

Turn fabric inside out. *See photo 71.* Insert cushion and blind stitch top edges with invisible thread and a curved needle. This is a very easy method for boxed cushions and the corners are very sharp. *See photo 72.*

67

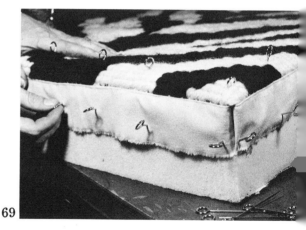

69

68

70

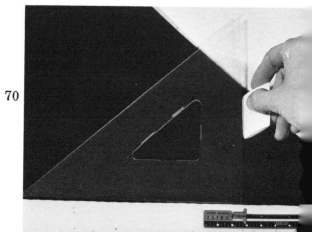

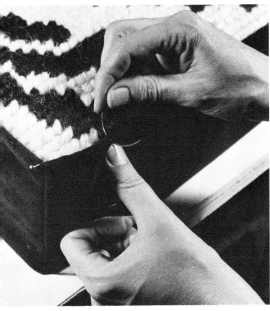

71

72

ROUND BOLSTER

See photo 73. Block needlework as required. Make enough *bias cording* to fit around both ends. *Apply bias cording* to face of needlework. Determine width of bolster and cut two strips of fabric one-half of this measurement plus a 1″ seam allowance. Machine stitch a strip to each end of the bolster. Fold over ½″ of the ends to the back of fabric and machine stitch to make casing. Thread narrow tape through these casings on each end. Fold the whole thing in half, right sides together and machine stitch the entire length, casing line to other casing. Pull narrow tape at one end and tie tight. Insert bolster and tie the other end tight. Tuck loose ends of tape inside. If you like, make a fabric covered button of the same fabric and sew to the center of each end.

73

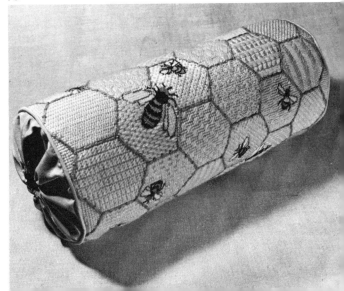

Dog Coat

Block needlework by the required method and allow it to dry.

Prepare a length of double-fold bias from the lining fabric. (See page 28.) This piece must be long enough to go around the outer edges of the assembled back of coat and under section.

Cut remaining lining fabric the same shape as the needlepoint pieces but allow a ½″ seam allowance on the center back. Sew the two halves of the lining together and press the seam open.

Sew the two back section pieces of the needlepoint together. *See photo 74.* To do this, fold the center seam allowance under and pin the two pieces, center edges together, flat on the blocking board. Begin blind stitching at the neck edge with invisible thread and a curved needle. (See page 24.)

Pin the lining and needlepoint together with right sides out. Machine stitch ¼″ inside the edge of the needlepoint. Trim lining and canvas right to the edge of the needlepoint. Either

machine zig-zag stitch over this cut edge or sew another two rows of straight stitches between the first row of stitches and the cut edge.

Begin stitching the bias strip at the seam of the neck curve. Open ½ fold of bias, place right sides together at edge and stitch on the first fold line. Fold ends of bias at meeting point and stitch across. *See photo 75.* Turn coat over, fold bias to the underside (over the edge) and pin to the lining. Hand stitch the folded bias edge to the coat lining. The under section is made the same way.

Mark position for snaps. (See page 35.) *See photo 76.* Apply snaps and give the coat a final light steaming. *See photo 77.*

74

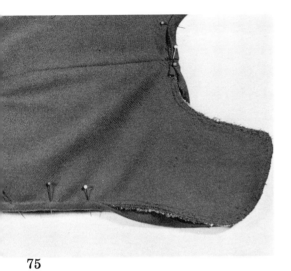

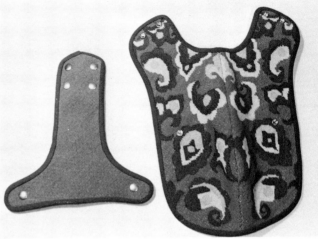

75

76

77

Brick Doorstops

UPHOLSTERED DOORSTOP

Block needlework by method required. *See photo 78.* Pad all sides of the brick with dacron batting or a ½" thick piece of polyfoam. Stitch the padding in place with rather long stitches. Sew corners of the needlepoint on the inside by machine or on the outside with the binding stitch. Crewel or other embroidery should be machine stitched. Trim seams to about ½". Spread seams apart and apply latex glue to raw edges so they will not ravel. Allow glue to dry.

Turn cover right side out and force needlework over padded brick. *See photo 79.* Fasten needlework cover in place with long herringbone stitches.

Cut fabric for bottom of brick about 1½" to 2" larger than base of doorstop. *See photo 80.* Turn edges under and pin in place with large pins. Use invisible thread and a curved needle to blind stitch base fabric to needlework. If cover is made of needlepoint, sew over

78

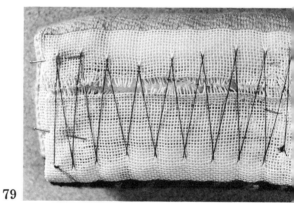

79

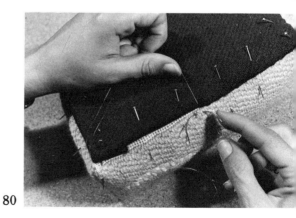

80

the last row of needlepoint stitches. Make sure you pick up the threads of the canvas and not just the wool thread. *See photo 81.*

BARN DOORSTOP

Block needlework as required and size if necessary. Corner and top seams are worked with the binding stitch on the outside so they will be sharp.

Measure the length, width and height from the top of the brick to the peak of the barn or house. Cut a triangular piece of styrofoam to these measurements. *See photo 82.* Smooth all edges and bottom with a wood file, sandpaper or the kind of coarse file used to remove corns. *See photo 83.* Glue the properly shaped styrofoam to the top of the brick. Allow to dry thoroughly.

Force the needlework cover over the brick. You may have to remove it and file the styrofoam a little more for a perfect fit. The cover must be snug over the brick. Secure the needlework to the bottom of the brick with long herringbone stitches.

Cut fabric for bottom of brick 1½″ to 2″ larger than the base of the barn. Turn raw edges under the pin in place. Use invisible thread and a curved

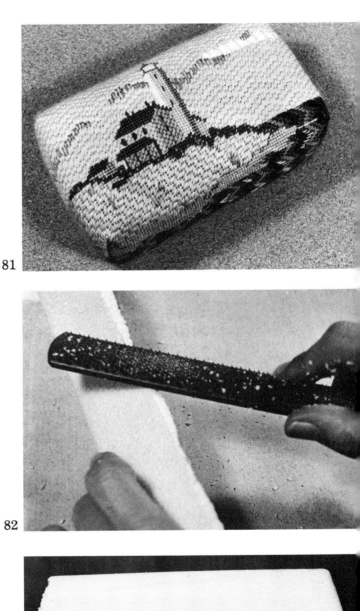

81

82

83

needle to blind stitch fabric to the needlework. If the barn is worked in needlepoint, sew over the last row of needlepoint stitches picking up canvas threads and not just wool threads. Give it a light final steaming to sharpen the edges. *See photo 84.*

HINTS: Most bricks have to be cleaned before use. Remove surface dirt with a brush and finish cleaning it in an electric dishwasher if you have one. You can put it through the drying cycle several times. I've found it best not to let my husband see this strange operation.

84

Fly Swatter

Try to find a fly swatter with a wire handle. The plastic handles break too easily.

Block and size needlepoint. Leave it on the blocking board until dry.

Cut surplus canvas away to within ¾ " from edge of needlepoint. *See photo 85.* Mitre corners and fold edges over leaving one row of unworked canvas. Work binding stitch in this row on all sides. Turn over to right side and steam on the blocking board again. *See photo 86.* Place the pins between the needlepoint stitches so they will not leave marks. Allow to dry.

Cut oil cloth or flexible plastic slightly larger than the finished needlepoint. With right sides out and needlepoint uppermost, begin machine stitching at one side of the handle opening and across the top. Leave the machine needle through your work and put the fly swatter between the oil cloth

85

86

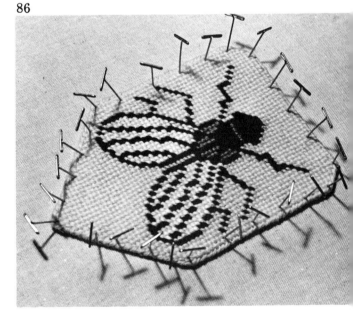

and needlepoint. Continue stitching down the last side to the handle. *See photo 87.* This line of stitching should be done just between the row of bind-ing stitch and the first row of needle-point. Use invisible thread. *See photo 88.* Trim the oil cloth close to the line of machine stitching.

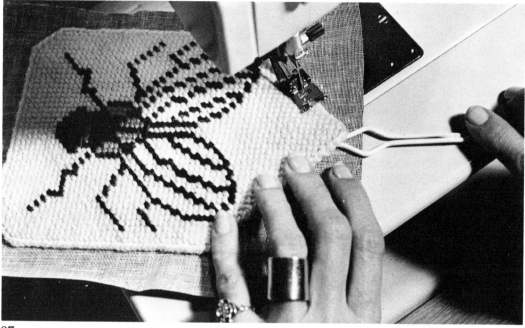

87
88

Footstools

ROUND
SLIP-SEAT
FOOTSTOOL

Dampen your needlework using the "London" method. Pin out on a blocking board to smooth stitches and allow it to get almost dry. Separate the base of the stool from the padded top. These two parts usually screw together from the under side. Remove the needlework from the blocking board while it is still slightly damp and cut away the surplus canvas to within about 2″ of the finished needlework.

Find the exact center of your stool top and the center of your design. Put a long pin through the center point of the design and into the center of the stool pad to secure it. Lay these on a flat, sturdy surface with the needlework facing down.

The first four rust-proof tacks or staples are to keep the needlework in position. Locate the straight-of-grain of the canvas or embroidery on each side and fasten it to the back of the pad at opposing points. *See photo 89.* Begin

working between two of the tacks where the fabric is on the bias. Pull the canvas to ease the needlework as much as possible. When you have worked out a bit of ease, and pulling tightly, put in a staple or tack about ½″ from the edge of the pad. Continue pulling and tacking every ¾″ until the whole section is as smooth as you can get it. *See photo 90.* If the needlework

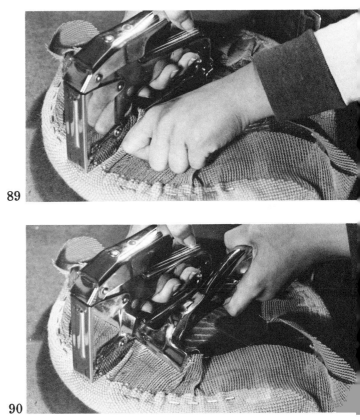

89

90

69

has a very tight tension you will find using canvas pliers a great help. Ease and tack the next section opposite the first one you have completed. Continue until all four sections have had every bit of ease removed at the edge of the pad. Allow pad to dry. The needlework will shrink slightly for a tighter fit as it is drying. *See photo 91.* Steam the surplus canvas down flat before you trim it away to about ¾″.

91

You may put a piece of upholsterers muslin over the bottom if you like. Staple it to the edge about every four or five inches. You can also sew it on with a very long running stitch.

After the stool is thoroughly dry, spray the top with a soil resistant product several times. (See page 12.) Allow it to dry again and attach it to the base. *See photo 92.* Putting the pad back on is easier if the screw locations have been marked on the back of the pad before the needlework is attached.

92

OBLONG FOOTSTOOL

This stool cover has been filled in with needlepoint at the corners. I sometimes do this if I'm not certain I want to leave it mounted as a stool.

Block needlework by the "London" method. Do not allow it to dry thoroughly on the board as you will be working with it slightly damp. As it dries it will shrink a little for a tighter fit.

This type of stool usually has a wooden insert that you have to pad yourself. This insert rests on a ridge just inside the top of the stool. Use 4″

thick polyfoam and mark it on all sides with a felt-tipped pen to the exact size of the wooden insert. *See photo 93.* Cut the polyfoam on these lines with an electric carving knife. Lay the foam over the wooden insert and secure it in place with a few strips of double-sided masking tape. Place the needle-point over it. Turn the whole thing upside down.

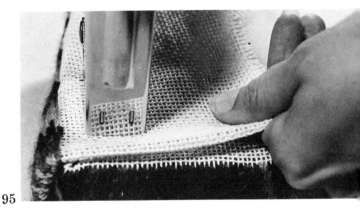

94

Use rust-proof tacks or staples to fasten one lone side of the needlework to the wood. Staple right to the ends. Do the other side next. *See photo 94.* Start folding the first corner as though you were going to mitre half of it. Staple it in place. *See photo 95.* The next fold is on the straight-of-grain of the canvas, over the half mitre, with the surplus needlepoint tucked inside.

95

93

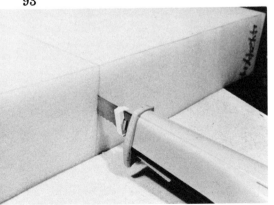

96

Staple this in place. Do the other corner the same way.

After the corners have been secured you can staple the canvas between so the edge of the needlework is even with the edge of the wooden insert. Do the other end the same way.

Allow the needlework to dry thoroughly. Spray it with a few coats of a soil-resistant product. *See photo 96.* Staple a piece of upholsterer's muslin to the under side. Give the tucked-under corners some steam and hand press them flat. Put it into its frame.

There is enough tension to the needlework fabric to round the top edges of the foam. If you don't want the stool as high or if your needlework does not allow it, upholster the wooden insert with a thinner piece of polyfoam. *See photo 97.*

97

Glass Cases

FOLDED GLASS CASE

Block and size the needlework. Cut away surplus canvas to within ½″ of edge of needlework. If your canvas or fabric ravels, apply latex glue on all edges at cutting line.

Lining Unit

Measure and cut an interlining of "Perma-Crin" ⅛″ smaller on all edges than the worked area of needlework. Measure and cut lining fabric (silk) ½″ larger on all sides than interlining. Fold top edge of lining over edge of interlining and adhere with latex glue.

Fold unit in half with lining inside and stitch down side and bottom right next to interlining. Open seams and press to back of interlining and adhere with latex. *See photo 98.*

Cover

Fold case in half to determine where long edges will join and mark the needlework at this point. Begin working binding stitch at lower top of edge of case. Continue working through the single edge until you reach your mark for joining. Fold the case in half and join the remainder of the two edges together with the binding stitch.

98

99

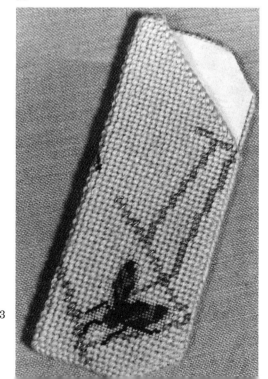

Slip lining unit into case and blind stitch the top edges of it to the binding stitch. Use invisible thread and a curved needle. Steam lightly if necessary. *See photo 99.*

TWO-PIECE GLASS CASE

Block needlework as required and give the wrong side a light coat of sizing. Trim canvas to ½" on both pieces. Apply latex cream to all edges and fold them to the inside. Try to have both pieces of needlework exactly the same size. Apply pressure to both pieces.

Lining Unit

Ultrasuede is used for the lining.

Cut two pieces of lining ¼" larger, on all sides, than the needlework. Lay the previously prepared needlework over a piece of lining and mark the outline of the needlework on the lining with tailor's chalk. Put the two pieces of lining together and machine stitch just inside of this mark on the long edges and across the bottom.

Cover

Use invisible thread and a curved needle to blind stitch the edges of the needlework to the outsides of the lining at the stitching line.

Steam flat and trim the edges of the Ultrasuede to ⅛" from edge of needlework. *See photo 100.*

100

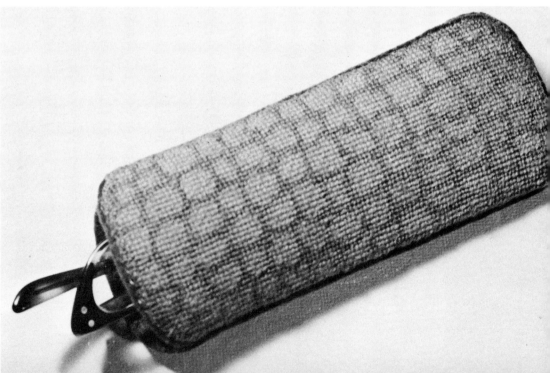

Ice Bucket

seams and machine stitch together wrong sides out. Press seam open. Butt edges of "Permette" and join on the inside with masking tape. *See photo 102.* Slip lining inside of "Permette"

Outside Cover

Measure inner circumference and height of ice bucket. Work the needle-point or crewel ⅛″ lower (height) and ¼″ shorter (circumference) than this measurement.

See photo 101. Pin seams of needle-point together at top and bottom and seam from the outside with invisible thread and a curved needle. (See page 24.) Press seam open.

Crewel or other embroidery may be machine stitched on the wrong side. Trim edges of needlework top and bottom into ½″. Fold this ½″ inside to first row of needlepoint or marked edge of crewel and press.

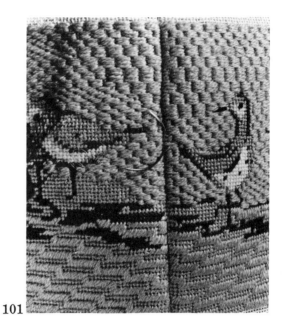

101

102

Lining Unit

Cut an interlining of "Permette" ¼″ lower (height) and ½″ shorter (circumference) than finished needle-work measurements. Lay the "Permette" interlining over the lining fabric. Cut the lining fabric 1″ larger on each edge. Mark ends of lining fabric for and fold lining edges over and press. Adhere folded edges of lining to outside of "Permette" with fusing tape and a warm iron or use latex glue.

Slip lining unit inside of needlework, attach top and bottom with the blind stitch, using invisible thread and a curved needle. *See photo 103*. Steam completed unit over a tailor's ham or rolled towel and pound the edges flat. Slip it into the bucket. At this point you may have to steam and

stretch it slightly for a perfect fit. *See photo 104*. Insert the plastic bucket liner firmly.

If you like the burlap texture of "Permette", eliminate the fabric lining. All you have to do is measure the "Permette", cut, butt the ends and join with masking tape on the inside. Turn in the edges of your needlework, slip it over the "Permette" and blind stitch the two together. Press and put it inside the ice bucket.

103

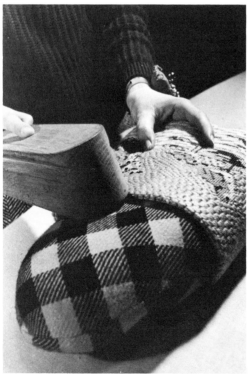

104

Jewelry Roll

Determine the desired finished size of the roll. Measurements for the one illustrated will be in parenthesis. (7″ x 11¼″) Work needlepoint one row larger than this measurement on all sides. Block face down and size with a medium-strength sizing solution. (See page 34.) Allow to dry thoroughly on the blocking board.

Trim surplus canvas to ¾″ on all edges. *See photo 105.* Apply latex cream to all exposed canvas. Fold these edges to the back and put under pressure (See page 34.) for about 20 minutes.

Interlining

Ultrasuede is used for the interlining and lining wherever they are mentioned.

Cut a piece of Ultrasuede at least ½″ wider and 4″ longer than needlepoint (7½″ x 15¼″). Now apply latex to the entire back of needlework. Start at the pointed end and smooth the Ultrasuede over the latex. You will have the extra 4″ of lining beyond the squared end of the needlepoint. Apply pressure and allow to set for about an hour.

Lining

Cut another piece of lining fabric 5¾″ shorter than the first piece (7½″ x 9¼″). Determine how far down from the top you want the zippered pocket (4″ to bottom of zipper opening). Mark the outline of this measurement with ruler and tailor's chalk. The opening for the zipper should be ½″ wide to within ½″ from both sides of the case (6″). Cut this opening out very carefully with sharp pointed scissors.

105

Center a 7″ zipper in the opening with the closed end of zipper at left side of opening. *See photo 106.* Fasten in place with zipper tape. Make sure the teeth of the zipper are centered in the opening. Stitch zipper in place on both long edges from the closed end of the zipper. (See page 35, #1.) Stitch across both short ends with the zipper closed.

106

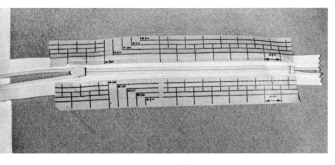

Ring Strap

Cut a 1″ strip of Ultrasuede for the ring strap (7″ x 1″). Fold in half and stitch down both sides and to a point at one end. Don't forget to start stitching at the same end for each side. Measure desired distance down from zipper for placement of the ring strap (2¼″), from bottom edge of zipper and even with the ends of zipper opening. Mark position for snap on pointed end of strap and on lining. Glue a ½″ x

½″ piece of "Permette", for reinforcement, under the mark for the bottom half of the glove snap. The mark for the top part of snap should be ½″ in from pointed end of the strap. Put the top half of the glove snap here. Attach the snap. Make a ½″ cut for the other end of the strap parallel to the side. Put the end of the strap through this cut and glue the short end in place on the back.

Flap for Lower Pocket

Measure the depth of the flap for the lower pocket (2″ deep). Mark these lines with tailor's chalk but do not cut. The sides of the flap should line up with the ends of the zipper and the ring strap. Locate the position of the snaps on the flap. Glue a ½″ x ½″ square of "Permette" under each location. Cut a backing strip of Ultrasuede ½″ deeper and the same width (total 2½″) as the flap. Lay the flap lining under the flap, hold it in place with zipper tape and stitch on the marked lines. Attach the tops of the glove snaps over your marks. Machine stitch around the edge of the flap. After everything is attached and sewn in place, trim the edges of the flap through both thicknesses with scissors.

Bottom Pocket

Go back to the piece of needle-work with the 4″ lining extension. Cut another piece of lining fabric the same measurement as the extension (4″ x 7½″). Glue this piece to the lining side of the extension. *See photo 107.* If you want to cut in ½″ for a neater finish to the pocket do so now. Machine stitch this edge, through both layers of lining. Mark position for lower portion of snap and attach it. *See photo 108.* Snap the pocket flap to the extension.

Final Steps

Fold the extension with its attached zipper and strap unit over. *See photo 109.* Apply double-sided sewing tape

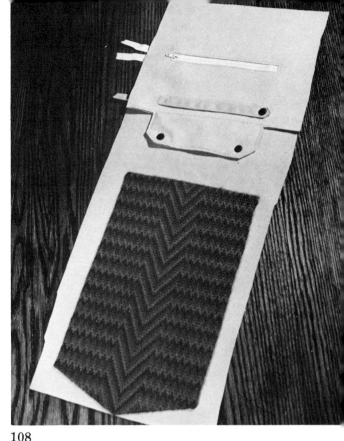

108
109

107

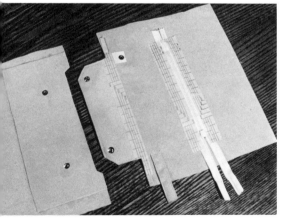

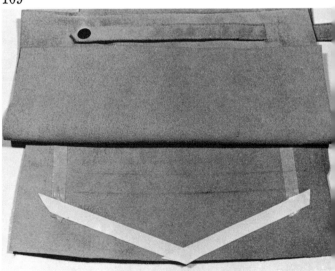

across the point between the two layers of Ultrasuede to hold everything in place. Begin machine stitching, with the needlework on top, at the point of the roll. Use the zipper foot, it is easier to keep close to the edge. Stitch the

110

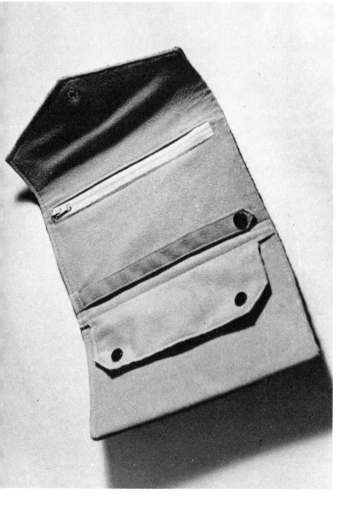

other edge in the same direction (starting at the point) and across the bottom. Use a sharp pair of scissors to trim all lining, surplus zipper and ring strap ends from the three edges of the roll. Turn the needlework over. Sew a row of machine stitching from edge to edge, across the roll, right on line with the bottom of the ring strap. Lock this row of stitching at both ends by lowering the machine feed and stitching in place three or four times. This row closes the bottom of the zippered pocket.

See photo 110. Mark position for closing snap on the point and attach it. Give the roll a final light bit of steam if it needs it. *See photo 111.*

111

Key Chains

Block needlework face down and size it with a medium solution. Cut surplus canvas to within ½″ of key-chain outline.

Cut one piece of interlining ("Permette") slightly smaller than the needlework. The needlepoint stitches must cover the edges of the interlining.

See photo 112. Block each piece separately over this piece of interlining with a little steam at the folded-over edges. Pin in place and allow to dry.

Apply latex cream to all edges of needlework. *See photo 113.* Work it into all surplus canvas right to last rows of background if keychain is needlepoint. Refold edges of needlework and sandwich the interlining between the coverings. Blind stitch edges together using invisible thread and a

112

curved needle. Steam and flatten after the two pieces are sewn together. Punch hole (see page 35) and affix a large eyelet. You can use either a chain or split ring to hold keys. *See photos 114, 115.*

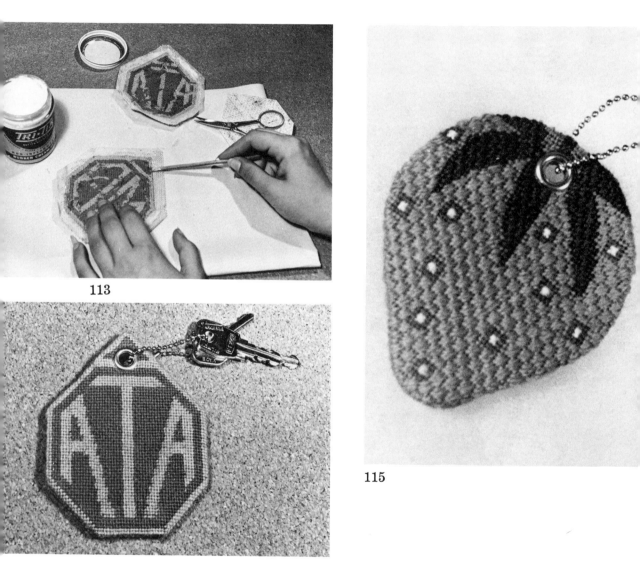

113

114

115

Needle Case

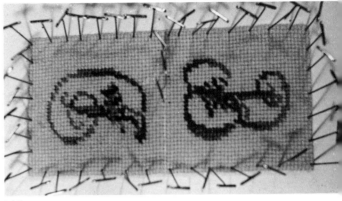

116

Outside Cover

Block needlepoint and apply latex to all edges at cutting line if your canvas ravels easily. Cut surplus canvas away to within ½″ of needlepoint edge. *See photo 116.* Fold edges under, block again and work binding stitch around all edges and down the center fold line. Steam lightly. Make sure your corners are square.

Lining Unit

Measure and cut "Perma-Crin" interlining ⅜″ smaller than finished needlework. Measure and cut silk lining ½″ larger on all sides than interlining. Make sure the lining is cut with the true grain of the fabric running parallel to edges. *See photo 117.* Press interlining flat, then press edges of lining over the interlining and mitre corners. You want good sharp edges. Apply a touch of latex glue under the mitred corners to hold them in place while you glue the edges. Apply glue sparingly. Hold down edges and run a thin

117

line of glue under each edge and press in place with your finger.

Cut a strip of interlining ⅜″ by about 1½″ long (this length depends on the size of your scissors). Cover with the same silk by folding the edges of the lining to the back and gluing this to the interlining but don't bother to mitre the corners. Just cut clean ends. Fold this strip in half, measure the space needed to insert the scissors and mark it here. Sew across the strip at this point. Next, mark the position on the lining where you want your scissors holder. Use dressmakers chalk as it brushes off easily. This line should be exactly the same measurement as the width of the strip you have just made. Before you cut this opening, sew one row of small stitches close to and all around this line with matching or invisible thread. *See photo 118.* Use a razor blade or very sharp knife to cut between the two rows of stitching all the way through the lining and inter-lining. From the right side, slip the scissors strip through the slot you have just made. Spread the ends apart on the back. Glue in place. Stitch in place on both sides of strip from the right side. *See photo 119.* Finger press the scissors holder flat to cover the stitch-ing.

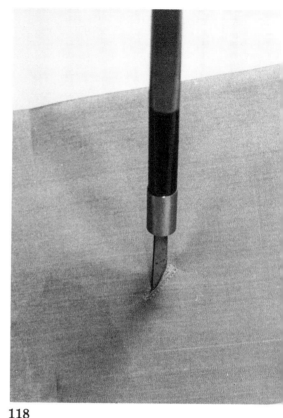

118

119

Use dressmakers pencil to mark exact position on your lining unit for the snaps. Attach snaps. Measure and cut two or three pieces of flannel or felt to fit between the snaps. Fold the flannel or felt in half and mark this fold line. Fold lining in half and mark this fold line also. *See photo 120.* Stitch through all layers down the center on the marked lines.

Pin this lining unit inside to the needlework at both ends. You will notice it is slightly shorter than the needlework. Pin to all edges easing the needlework towards the center. *See photo 121.* Blind stitch lining unit to outside cover on all edges using invisible thread and a curved needle. Fold in half, snap and give it a final light steaming.

Crewel Embroidery, Cross Stitch, etc.

Simply cut needlework ½″ larger than required size on all sides. Cut interlining of "Perma-Crin" to exact finished measurement. Center interlining on wrong side of embroidery. Fold ½″ allowance over edges of interlining and press in place. Glue these edges to the back with latex. Proceed to make lining unit and insert as in above directions.

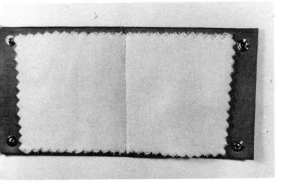

120
121

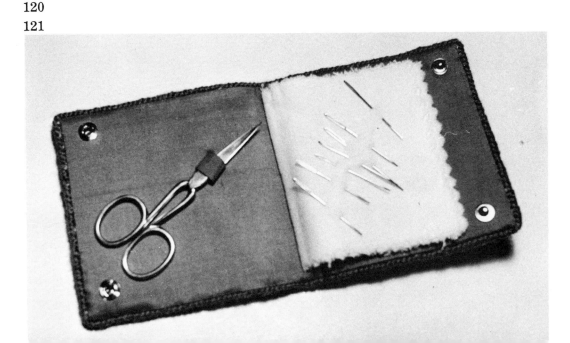

Pictures

UNFRAMED MAT

Velvet is used here but silk or any suitable material may be used.

Cut mounting cardboard to required size. Center the board over the velvet on the wrong side. *See photo 122.* Apply 1″ masking tape to under side of velvet on one edge leaving ½″ of the sticky side exposed. Apply 2″ masking tape over this on right side of velvet, to fasten to board. Continue with each edge in this manner. If you prefer, you may simply fold the edges of the velvet to the back of the board and adhere it to the back with latex.

Cut backing fabric ½″ larger than board. Turn under all edges ½″ and pin in each corner to the board. *See photo 123.* Blind stitch the edge of backing fabric and edge of velvet-covered board together using invisible thread, curved needle and blind stitch. *See photo 124.* Sew a ribbon across the back ⅓ of the way from the top for hanging. Of course you don't need the ribbon if you are going to place the needlework on a small table easel.

Block and size needlework. Cut mounting cardboard to required size. Needlepoint stitches should fold around to cover edges. Adhere fabric or canvas to back of the board with masking tape or latex cream.

Position needlework on velvet-covered board with a pin at each corner. Blind stitch in place. *See photo 125.*

122

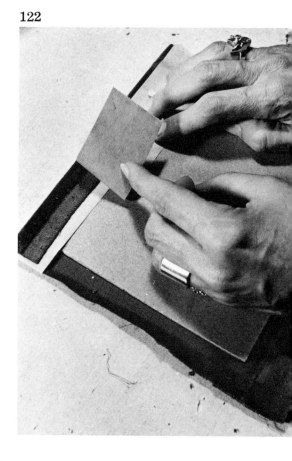

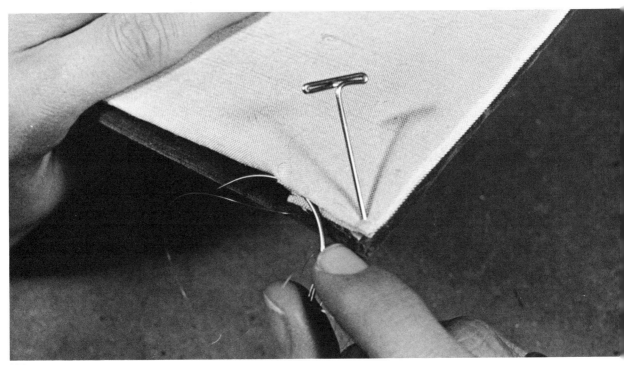

123

124

OVAL PICTURES

Select proper size frame. Cut oval mounting board about ¼″ smaller than inside of frame to allow for thickness of fabric. Block needlework as required. Center embroidery within the oval from the right side. Secure one side in two or three places with pins. Bring top and bottom edges of needlework over to the back of the mat. Hold in place with push pins. Apply thin sizing (see page 34), as a paste, liberally to underside of embroidery and back of mounting board with a brush. Paste will saturate linen. It should be wet to within ½″ of turned edge. *See photo 126.* Take small tucks and pin in place to back of mounting board. Allow to dry thoroughly. You may use a hair dryer to hasten drying. Never use just heat alone. Always have some blowing air with heat. Let this side dry thoroughly and remove your pins and continue with the other side in exactly the same manner.

After needlework is completely dry on back, place it in your frame. Either put in small finishing nails or glazier's diamonds to hold your embroi-

125

dery in place in the frame. Cut a piece of plain wrapping paper the same shape but ¼″ smaller than your frame. Dampen this lightly with a wet sponge so it will shrink. Glue this to the back of your frame with the same rice size. Attach the type of hanger you desire. *See photo 126.*

If you want to remove it at a later date, just lay a damp cloth over the back long enough to loosen the glue. It will remove very easily.

NEEDLEPOINT

Liquid latex, instead of rice size, is applied to edge of canvas and allowed to dry. Slash canvas to within ¼″ of folded edge every ½″. Apply latex glue to mounting board and finger-press the canvas in place.

Note: I have left a lot of surplus linen on the back of this picture because I am not certain I will always want it as originally planned. The sizing washes out easily and I can always remount it a different way if I choose to in the future.

Rectangular pictures are either sewn over mounting board (see page 86) or fastened to the board with masking tape.

126

Rugs

Work rugs on a frame if possible. It is important that the stitch count is accurate on the edge of all pieces of rugs worked in sections.

Dampen rugs using the "London" method. They are usually left on the blocking board two or three days after they are dry. Canvas pliers are almost always necessary.

Large stitch canvas has a tendency to ravel so allow wide margins of un-worked canvas. After the rug has been blocked and dried you can apply latex glue to the raw edges of the canvas if they are unraveling.

Upholsterer's canvas is used to interline rugs and an even-weave "Herculon" is used for the lining. I find burlap very unsatisfactory because the weave is not close enough to stabilize the rug and it has an objectionable odor in damp weather.

If the rug creeps out of shape after blocking you will have to apply the interlining as for round rugs page 131.

Needlepoint rugs are usually laid over a non-slip padding.

Give all rugs several light coats of a good silicone soil-resistant spray.

127

ONE-PIECE RECTANGULAR RUG

Dampen rug by "London" method. Block on large piece of insulation board. *See photo 127*. Square corners and straighten sides with a large T-square. Sometimes this process must be repeated two or three times before you let it dry. *See photo 128*. Edges will wear better if the binding stitch is applied after the first blocking.

128

Interlining

Cut the canvas interlining ½" smaller on all edges than the finished measurement of the rug. Lay the interlining over the back of the rug on top of the blocking board and pin in place every 6 or 8 inches. *See photo 129.* Use a curved needle and invisible thread to tack the interlining with 4 or 5 inch running stitches. Try to catch just the back of the rug with your needle. Since you are using invisible thread stitches won't show if you go all the way through occasionally. Work from end to end then from one side to the other. Don't pull these running stitches too tight.

Mitre corners. Turn unworked edges of canvas over the edge of the interlining and secure with long herringbone stitches. *See photo 130.* You can use ordinary carpet thread for these stitches. Steam the edges flat.

Lining

Cut the lining fabric 1" larger than the rug on all sides. Lay the lining over the rug (right side up), fold edges

129

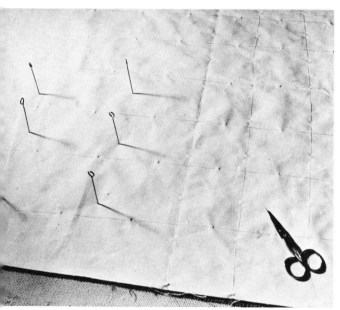

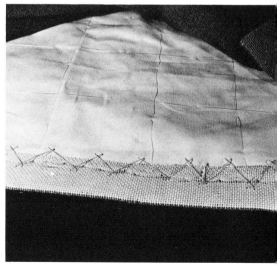

130

under and pin in place. Use a curved needle and invisible thread to blind stitch lining to edge of rug. Be sure you pick up needlepoint canvas and not just wool threads when you stitch.

Pin out on your blocking board again with the pins about 3 or 4 inches apart. Give the whole rug a final light steaming.

PIECED RUGS

Each piece is dampened and blocked separately. Pay particular attention to exact measurements of each piece.

Lay pieces out (face up) on blocking board. Fold seams under and blind stitch sections together from the right side with invisible thread and a curved needle. (See page 24.)

Use steam to block the entire rug, face up, after all seams have been sewn. Go on to interline and line the rug as directed in preceding directions.

The above method was used apply the darker borders to the "Possum" rug. *See photo 131.*

ROUND OR OVAL RUGS

Cut (or have cut) a template of

131

insulating board to the exact shape
and size of the finished rug. An extra
½″ of needlepoint is worked around
the rug. This ½″ is turned under later.
The upholsterer's canvas interlining is
glued to the back of the rug with latex.

Dampen rug using the "London"
method. *See photo 132.* Use rust proof

tacks to fasten the rug to the edges of
the template.

Interlining

Use the template to cut out the
canvas interlining and lining. The canvas should be cut ½″ smaller than the

132

finished rug and the lining is cut 1″ larger than the finished rug. Draw a line around the template on the right side of the lining with tailor's chalk. *See photo 133.* Piece the canvas interlining with a flat over-lapped seam if necessary.

Lay the rug face down on a firm surface. Place the interlining over the back and fold the interlining half way back. *See photo 134.* Begin adhering the canvas to the back of the rug with latex cream. Brush the latex across the rug in a 2″ strip. Press the canvas over the latex and roll (see page 33) firmly. Proceed to the lower edge in

this manner. Finish glueing the other half of the rug from the center to the edge. Put the template over the canvas. Put some heavy weight on top and allow to dry thoroughly.

See photo 135. Turn the edges of the rug over the canvas interlining. Steam to remove surplus and trim needlepoint canvas to 2″. Glue the needlepoint canvas to the interlining. Let this edge dry. Lay the lining over the rug. Slash lining edges to within ¼″ of the chalk line (finished edge) and fold under here. Pin in place and use a curved needle and invisible thread to sew the lining to the needlepoint.

See photo 136. Turn the rug over and work fringe and trim it evenly.

133

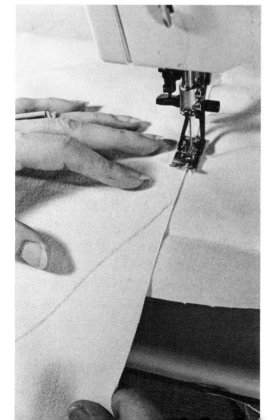

134

Sandals

Order the wooden soles (see Sources for soles, cement and nails) as you need them for measurements. The soles have been lightly sanded and sprayed with several coats of clear varnish. Ultrasuede is used for lining.

Work straps by folding canvas edges to center back and stitching design through both layers of canvas to within one row of edges. Work binding stitch on all edges of straps. Length of straps depends on foot size. The short straps for the toe section are 1″ wide. Instep straps are 1¾″ wide. *See photo 137.*

Cut "Ultrasuede" for each strap, the same size. Spread cement to back

of straps, position lining and apply pressure for about 1 hour.

Ultrasuede is applied to the tops of the wooden soles with cement and pressed into place. Allow to dry over night. Trim the edges as neat as possible. This lining stops your foot from slipping forward if you decide to wear stockings with the sandals. *See photo 138.*

138

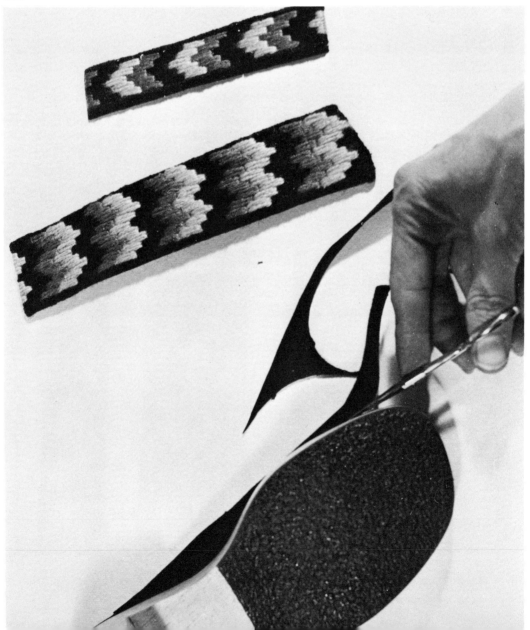

Give yourself a fitting for strap placement. The bottom edge of the lower strap should cross your foot where the base of the toes bend. Mark this position on the edge of sole with a pencil. Place the instep strap high enough on your foot to keep the sole from flopping. Mark this point with a pencil. Glue straps in place and allow them to dry thoroughly before nailing.

Nail the straps in place with long sole nails. Space them in pairs with room enough between nail heads to push in decorative upholsterer's tacks. *See photo 139.* Each wide strap end needs six sole nails and three decorative tacks. Narrow straps require four sole nails and two tacks.

139

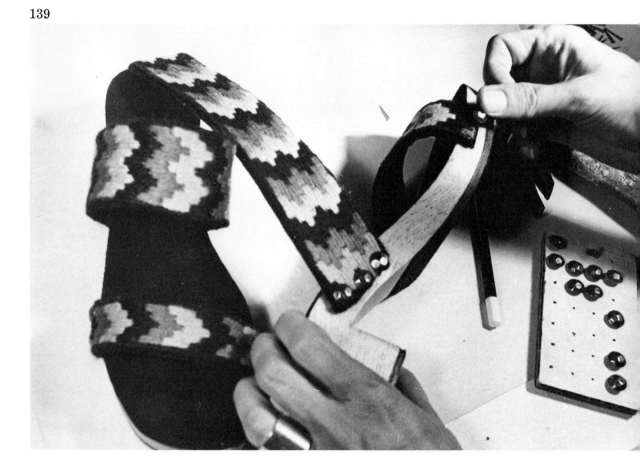

Toe Stuffers and Pincushions

TOE STUFFERS

See photo 140. Block by method required. Cut canvas to within ½″ of needlepoint. Cut a piece of fabric for the back this exact shape and size.

Put the needlepoint and fabric right sides together. Machine stitch around the edges just within the needlepoint leaving an opening in the top (about 1½″). Turn and stuff. You can save your wool clippings from your needlepoint for this or purchase lamb's wool from a drug store.

Turn raw edges to the inside, pin and sew opening together with invisible thread.

Stems can be made of braided yarn, twisted cord (see page 33) or purchased cord. Sew them in place with invisible thread.

The strawberry can be used for a pincushion also.

PINCUSHION

Block needlepoint as required. Pincushions are made exactly the same as larger cushions (see Cushions). The cording can be made of ribbon over a fine string. Use light weight fabrics like silk, cotton moiré or dressmaker's velveteen. Stuff them with wool clippings from your needlework or purchase lamb's wool from the drug store.

140

Wall Hangings

This wall hanging was worked in half-cross stitch but because it was done on a tapestry frame it needed only a little steam when it was blocked. Try to work all hangings on a frame.

Upholsterer's denim is used for the interlining and natural linen is on the back.

Block hanging by required method, face down. Brush a medium sizing solution over the entire back and allow to dry. Unpin the edges and leave it on the blocking board for about a week to see if it is going to creep out of shape. If it does, you will have to glue the interlining to the back with latex (see Round rug lining, page 95).

Interlining

Cut the denim ½″ smaller, on all sides, than the finished hanging. Lay the interlining over the back and pin in place. Use a curved needle and invisible thread to sew the interlining to the back with long, loose running stitches. These lines of stitches are about 5″ apart and run from top to bottom. *See photo 141.* Fold the edges of the needlepoint canvas over to the back. Mitre the corners and sew the canvas to the denim with carpet thread and the herringbone stitch. Steam the edges flat.

141

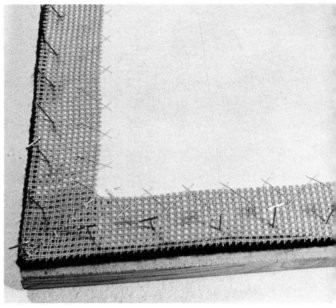

Loops

Make loops of needlepoint, linen, twisted cord or purchased braid. Attach them, evenly spaced, along top back edge with invisible thread.

Lining

Cut lining fabric 1″ larger, on all sides, than the hanging. Fold lining edges under and pin in place. Sew lining to edge of hanging with invisible thread and a curved needle.

See photo 142. Give the hanging a final light steaming if it needs it. Slip the rod through the loops and hang. You can make a twisted cord (see page 33) to match a color within the hanging if you like. Tie the ends of the cord to the ends of the rod and hang with a decorative hanger.

Give it several light coats of a silicone spray. Vacuum the hanging, whenever necessary, with the upholstery brush attachment to your vacuum cleaner.

142

Scissors Case

This case is constructed of two pieces of needlework joined together. Measurements of needlework should be one-half inch larger than desired finished size of required inside dimensions. You will lose approximately one-quarter inch in seams.

Block needlework face down and apply a light sizing solution to the back. Allow it to dry thoroughly. Cut surplus canvas to within one-quarter inch of needlework. Apply rubber cream to all edges. Fold canvas and one row of needlework to the back and apply pressure for about ten minutes. Both pieces should match around the bottom edges.

Cut Ultrasuede lining pieces slightly larger than needlework. Apply rubber cream to entire back of needlework. Position lining on back and apply pressure for at least one hour. Trim edges of lining close to edge of needlework.

Mark position for small pieces of Velcro and pin them in place. Machine stitch with either matching or invisible thread. *See photo 143.* You can use snaps here if you prefer. Join the two pieces of needlework with lining sides facing inside. Machine stitch together one-eighth inch from the edge. Begin stitching at the bottom center and sew toward the opening. Lock your thread at the end by stitching in place two or three times. Sew the other edge the same way, beginning at the bottom center and stitch to the opening.

Use two threads of the same yarn in the needlework to make the fine cord for the edges. To do this, anchor these threads on the edge, at the center bottom or side, and trim stray ends. Twist

143

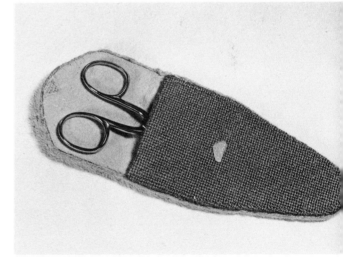

the threads of the yarn as you blind stitch it to the edge. Use either matching or invisible thread. *See photo 144.*

Fold the flap over and give it a final light steaming. *See photo 145.* If

you have used snaps, insert the top half of the snap last.

Scissors cases may be made in one piece and lined with fabric the same as the folded glass case. *See page 73.*

144

145

Cosmetic Cases

TWO POCKETS-ZIPPERED

Work two pieces of needlework to the desired size. This case measures 6½ inches by 4 inches. It has two pockets, one open and one zippered. The back section is worked long enough to fold over and snap to the approximate center of the front section to hold things in the pocket that does not have a zipper.

Block both pieces of needlework right side down and apply a medium sizing solution to the backs. When sizing is dry, trim surplus to ½ inch and apply rubber cream around all edges on back of needlework. Fold surplus canvas and one row of needlework to the back. Cover with waxed paper and apply pressure for about 25 minutes.

Lining

Cut *two* pieces of Ultrasuede slightly larger than the small, front piece of needlework. Cut one piece of Ultrasuede slightly larger than the longer back section with the flap. Apply rubber cream over the entire backs of the two pieces of needlework. Place the linings in position and apply pressure for at least one hour. You will notice you have an extra piece of lining. Put it aside for the present.

Remove needlework from pressure boards and trim linings even with needlework edges. Insert bottom half of snap in the approximate center of the front piece.

Machine stitch needlework to one half of the opened zipper, ⅛ inch in from the top edge of the front. Stitch

146

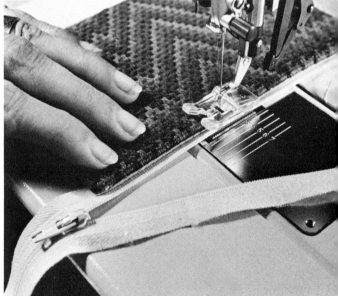

with the needlework on top. Inserting the zipper is easier if your zipper is about two inches longer than the needlework so the slide is beyond the stitching area. *See photo 146*. Now take the extra piece of lining and stitch it over the zipper tape just as you stitched the needlework to the first half of the zipper. Begin stitching at the same end.

Push the zipper slide to the center. Fold back lining at center of zipper and pin it to the edges of the needlework. Trim lining and zipper ends even with edges. Line up this section with the back and beginning at the bottom edge, machine stitch through all layers. *See photo, 147*. Stop stitching after you sew over the zipper ends and lock your threads by stitching in the same place a few times. Stitch the other end closed the same way. Remember to stitch from the bottom edge toward the zipper and on the same side of the needlework. *See photo 148*. Stitch across the bottom last.

Position the top half of the snap on the flap and insert. *See photo 149*. Lightly steam the fold and spray it with a soil resistant product.

147

148

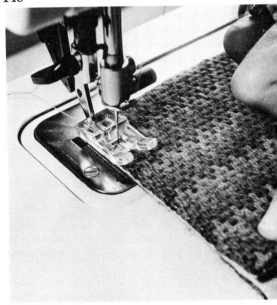

ONE POCKET-WITHOUT FLAP

To make a plain zippered case, without the flap, you would make the two pieces of needlework exactly the same measurements. Block, size the needlework and cut only two pieces of Ultrasuede lining. Glue the lining to the needlework as in above directions. Open the zipper and sew the two pieces of needlework to each half of the zipper. Close the zipper to the center and stitch both side edges from the bottom. Sew across the bottom edge last.

149

Checkbook Cover

Work needlepoint two inches longer and ¾ inches wider than your checks. Block right side down and apply a heavy sizing solution to the back. Allow to dry. Trim unworked canvas to within ½ inch of needlework, fold these edges to the back and glue in place with rubber cream. Make sure you fold one row of needlepoint to the back also. Apply pressure for about 20 minutes.

Cut a piece of Ultrasuede slightly larger than your needlework. Apply rubber cream to the entire back of needlework. Place the lining in position and apply pressure for at least one hour. Cut another piece of Ultrasuede four inches shorter and the same width as the other piece of lining. Place this piece of lining 2¾ inches from the fold-over end. Have the needlework on top to stitch through all layers, down the long sides. *See photo 150.* Don't forget to start stitching from the same end on both edges. Trim away surplus lining. *See photo 151.* Stitch across the short ends. Determine where the center fold

150

151

108

line is and stitch across all layers on the right side. *See photo 152.*

Fold cover and steam lightly. Finger press the folds while they are still damp. Mark position for snaps and insert them. Checks will slip into one end and you have a pocket in the other end. *See photo 153.*

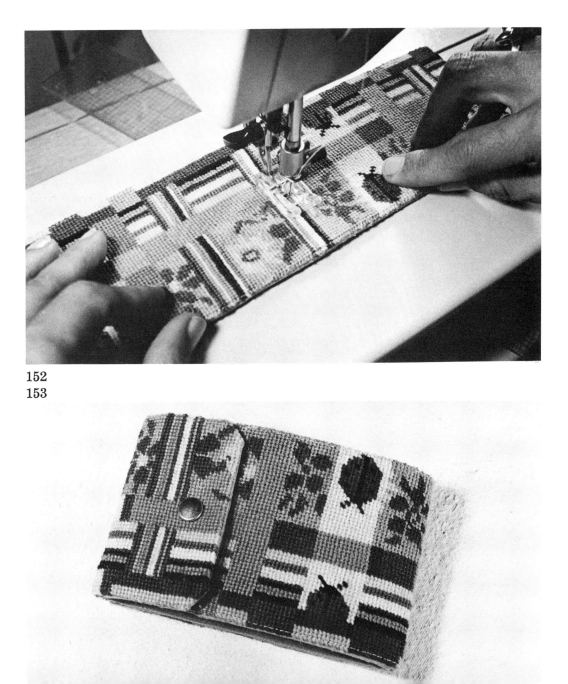

152
153

Drapery Tie-Back

Needlepoint, crewel or other fabrics are covered the same way. Block needlework as required. Cut interlining of a stiff, light-weight fabric (Perma-Crin was used here) ¼ inch smaller than desired finished size.

Work on your blocking or ironing board. Position interlining on wrong side and steam edges of needlework over the interlining. *See photo 154.* Trim edges of needlework to about one-half inch. If the outside is needlepoint, you can glue these edges in place if you choose to.

Cut lining material one inch larger than the tie-back. Fold edge of lining under as you pin it in place over the tie-back. Place bone or metal rings between lining and tie-back at each end and pin these in place also. *See photo 155.*

Use a curved needle and invisible thread to blind stitch the lining in place while it is still pinned to the board. Give it a final light steaming on the right side. *See photo 156.*

154

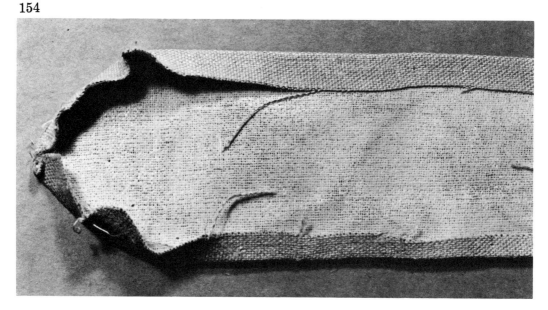

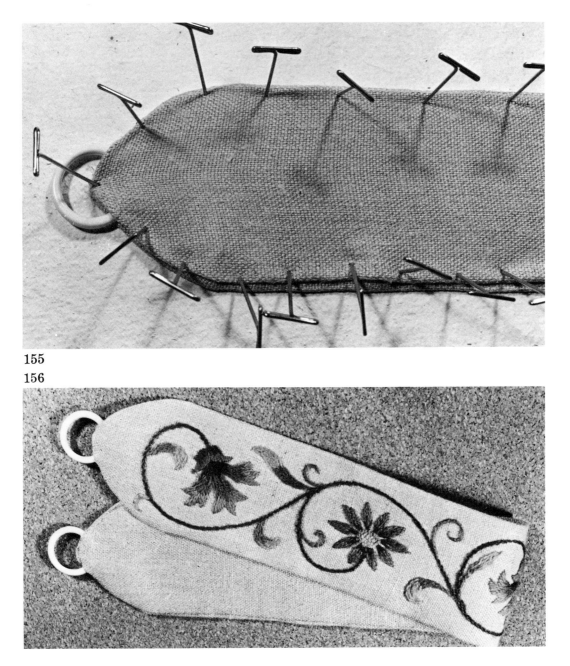

155
156

Handbag

Work front and back of needle-point to desired shape and size. Work an additional piece long enough to fit down both sides and across the bottom.

Block as required and apply a heavy sizing solution to the backs of the needlework pieces. Allow to dry. Trim surplus canvas to within one-half inch of needlework and join pieces with the binding stitch. *See photo 157.*

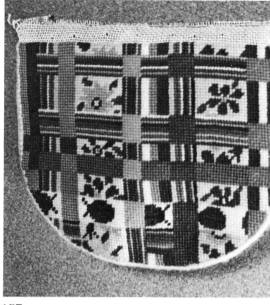

157

Interlining

Use Perma-Crin for small bags and cardboard (not corrugated) for larger bags. Cut front, back and side strip. These should be one-quarter inch smaller on all edges than needlework. Try a piece inside the cover to make sure it fits easily. Join interlining pieces together with strong masking tape. *See photo 158.*

158

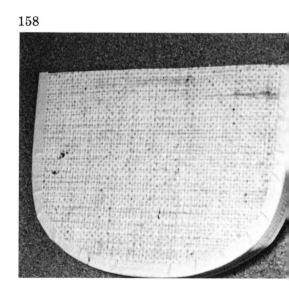

Lining

Cut fabric pieces one-half inch larger than interlining pieces. If you want an inside pocket, stitch this in place on the lining now. Just cut pocket twice the size needed plus one-quarter inch seams on outside edges. Fold piece in half and press. Fold raw edges under and press. Pin to lining at corners of pocket and stitch in place on sides and bottom. Machine stitch lining pieces together with ¾ inch seams. Try it inside the interlining to make sure it fits snugly. *See photo 159.*

Insert lining section into interlining. Fold edges of lining over edges of interlining and glue in place. Put the inner section into the needlework cover. Fold surplus canvas edges to the inside and pin the needlework to the lining section.

Insert large eyelets at each end, one-quarter inch from top edge, through all layers. Fasten ends of chain handle through the eyelets.

Zipper

Use zipper two inches longer than the opening. Cut one length of Ultrasuede one inch wider and one inch longer than opening. Cut this piece in half lengthwise. Open zipper and machine stitch one piece of Ultrasuede to each half of the zipper. Don't forget to start stitching at the same end of the zipper on each side. Push zipper

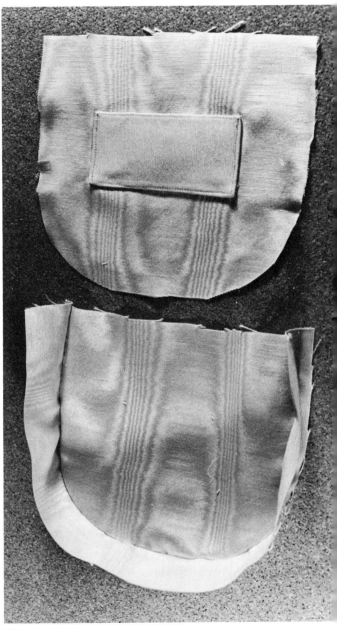

159

slide up a short distance and trim surplus tape at each end.

Unpin the edges of the needlework from the lining and insert the zipper strip between the lining and needlework. Repin in place. Use invisible thread to blind stitch. Anchor your thread at one end of handbag. Pick up two threads of canvas, stab through Ultrasuede to the inside of the bag. Pick up a few threads of the lining and stab through the Ultrasuede to the right side. Continue blind, stab stitching until zipper is sewn in all the way around bag opening. *See photo 160.* Spray lightly with a soil resistant product.

160

Waste Basket

The needlework should measure the exact circumference of the container to be covered. Top and bottom measurements should be exact also.

Block needlework to exact measurements and apply a medium sizing solution to the back. Allow it to dry thoroughly. Cut away surplus canvas to one inch on all sides. Fold top and bottom areas of unworked canvas to the back and glue in place with rubber cream. Apply pressure for about 20 minutes. If you are using small pressure boards you will have to do one edge at a time.

Position needlework around container. Fold the seam allowances under and baste in place, on the right side, with large herringbone stitches. (See page 24.) Use invisible thread and a curved needle to blind stitch the seam with small, tight stitches. Spray lightly with a soil resistant product.

This method of covering a waste basket allows you to slip the cover off from the bottom for cleaning. *See photo 161.*

161

Cleaning and Restoration

If stains are quite extensive in any piece you can only wash the whole thing in "Woolite" or dry cleaning fluid. If you just have small spotted areas try one of the following methods.

REMOVING MILDEW

Wait for a sunny day to do this but try to rinse the stain as soon as it is noticed. Treat the stains while they are fresh. The mold spores continue to grow and weaken the fabric. Use new 3% Hydrogen Peroxide as it loses its strength when stored for very long.

Saturate the *stains only*, use a medicine dropper to put the peroxide on the spots. Put the piece in bright sunlight and keep the stains saturated with peroxide until the spots disappear. This can take several hours. Run cold water from the faucet through the needlework until all of the peroxide is removed. If there are a lot of stains it is easier to just rinse the whole thing in cool water. Avoid this ever happening again by drying needlework in a well ventilated area but away from high heat.

You can also try a sodium perborate bleach and use the same method.

BLEEDING OR RUNNING COLORS

The only time this would be likely to happen is when the needlework is wet for blocking. Keep your eye on it for a little while after it has been placed on the blocking board. If you notice the slightest bleeding of colors, remove it from the blocking board immediately. Rinse in cold water. Keep rinsing in running cold water until a tissue or paper towel pressed on the offending color does not leave the slightest stain.

If you notice the stain after it is dry, try the peroxide method above. If this fails lemon juice will help sometimes.

GREASE STAINS

These stains are best removed with a good dry cleaning fluid. Lay a clean white towel on a kitchen counter top. Place the needlework, face down, over this. Pour a little of the cleaning fluid through the needlework. Press into the towel with your fingers, move the spot over a little (so it will be over a clean area) and repeat the process until the stain is removed.

Of course none of the above methods will work if the needlework is nailed down as on a chair seat. Try the dry cleaning method but press with toweling from the top instead of underneath. There is a product on the market for cleaning needlepoint in this position. It is called "Stitch Clean Needlepoint Cleaner." It works well but you have to clean the whole seat and sometimes this leads to cleaning all the seats if you have a spot on one of a matching pair or set. It is sprayed on and wiped off with wet terry cloth. Do not use it on cotton or silk.

RUST STAINS

Treat the stains with a 2% solution of Oxalic Acid or Hypo (photo developing solution) available from any photography shop. Rinse several times in clear, room temperature water. HINT: Wool absorbs liquid slowly so as soon as something is spilled, soak up the liquid with a clean absorbent cloth or blotter.

DRY OR WET CLEANING FRAGILE FABRICS

Dry cleaning is used in a different sense here as no liquid comes in contact with the fabric.

Make a support of fiberglass screen.

1: Cut a piece of screen several inches larger than the piece to be cleaned. Fold the screen in half.

2: Either hand stitch or zig-zag machine stitch, with nylon monofilament thread. Sew across short open end, down the open side and across the fold.

3: Lay the fabric inside this support and use long stitches to tack the delicate fabric inside.

Dry cleaning: Use a hand vacuum cleaner to draw all dust etc. from the front and back of the fabric. You can also use the hose attached to the blower end of your vacuum cleaner. Don't have the hose close enough to the fabric to damage it. Blow from the back of the fabric.

Wet Cleaning: Mix a weak solution of "Woolite". Fill a receptacle large enough to receive the entire piece (you might have to use the bath tub) with enough cleaning solution to cover the article well. Wash the piece very gently until the water appears dirty. Rinse

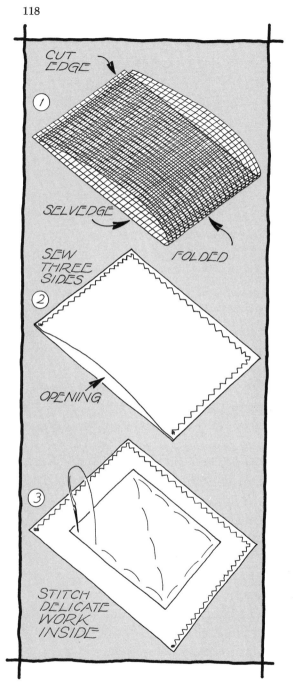

CUT EDGE

①

SELVEDGE

SEW THREE SIDES

②

FOLDED

OPENING

③

STITCH DELICATE WORK INSIDE

several times with clear water. Solution and rinse water should be room temperature. Let it dry in the support or gently smooth it onto a piece of glass (or the kitchen counter top) until it is dry.

ANTIQUE SILK NEEDLEPOINT

Because the acids in wood and cardboard have a detrimental effect on textiles, museum board is always used for mounting. It is certified 100% rag content and is guaranteed not to have any damaging chemicals in its composition. It is available only in a cream color, from custom framers.

Pin the needlework on the cut-to-size museum board. Lay a piece of nylon net on top of the needlework. Wet and ring out a piece of clean white terry cloth and put this on top of the net. Cover with a piece of plastic wrap. Keep checking the needlework to see when it is just damp enough to pull it gently into shape. Straighten the needlework and allow it to dry. *See photos 162, 163.* Fold the edges of the needlework to the back of the board and sew it in place. Place in the frame you have selected.

Since this piece of needlework is made of silk, a clean piece of flannel

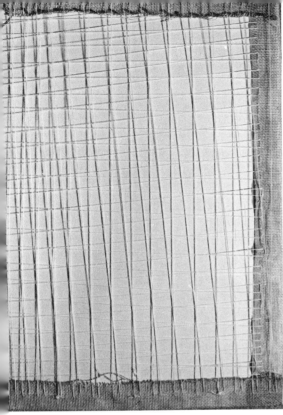

was glued to the back of the frame to keep out dust and gases, and to allow moisture from the atmosphere to reach the inside of the frame. This helps prevent dry rot. Do not glue paper to the back of the frame. Gently vacuum the back occasionally. If the silk is very old and dry rot has already started, place a clean piece of flannel over the museum board under the needlework before you sew it in place.

ANTIQUE SILK NEEDLE-MADE LACE

The idea here is to preserve the needlework, not to renew it.

See photo 164. The silk lining fabric was very carefully removed with

162

163

164

forceps. The wooden frame to which the lace was fastened was full of insect holes. *See photo 165.* Insecticide was injected into each hole. *See photo 166.* Next, powdered DDT was mixed with melted beeswax and forced into each hole. (This takes care of anything that might hatch in the future.) *See photo 167.* A replacement piece of China silk was cut and gently pushed between the edge of the frame and lace. A layer of flannel was cut to size and placed over this. Next, a thin layer of dacron batting (the depth of the frame) was

165

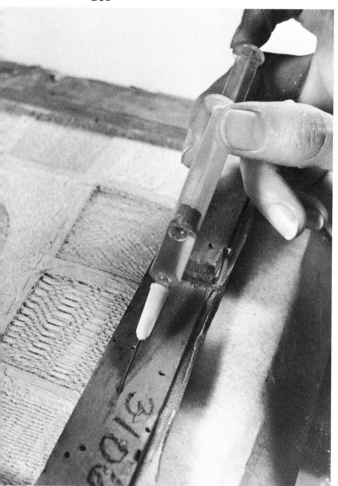

166

167

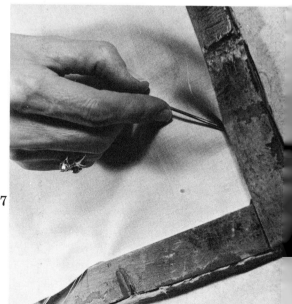

inserted. *See photo 168.* Everything is held in place with nylon net, glued to the edges of the frame with rice paste. *See photo 169.* Finally, a clean piece of flannel has been glued (rice paste also) to the back of the frame. No attempt was made to repair stitches, etc.

ANTIQUE WOOL NEEDLEPOINT

See photo 170. This piece is cross-stitch worked over canvas on a wool broadcloth fabric. The threads of the canvas were then removed or cut close to the edge of the needlepoint stitches. You can see the ends of some. The moths have been at it and the colors on the front are very faded.

First, it was supported in the fiberglass screen support and cleaned with cleaning fluid. It had a very objectionable odor after this so it had to air in

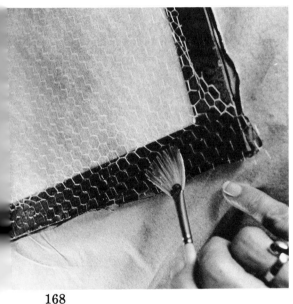

168

169

170

the support for about a week. It is simply sandwiched between two pieces of non-reflecting plexiglass with holes drilled in each corner of the plexiglass. It is fastened together with clear plastic binder posts through these holes. It rests on a plastic easel so it can be picked up for close inspection. The colors on the back have not faded and they are still bright and beautiful.

LION RUG

See photo 171. This was the first piece of needlepoint I ever worked (over 20 years ago). I did not use a frame and worked it in half cross stitch (a disaster!) with a rather poor quality yarn. It is 7″ on the bias at all corners (looks more like a triangle). It has been washed about 10 times and even dried in the clothes drier once. It looked so awful I didn't care what happened to it (but I couldn't throw it away) so it was hidden in the rag bag until my husband found it. He decided he liked it . . . Heaven forbid!!

First I washed it again and blocked

171

it face down. *See photo 172.* I ripped out the mane and fringes and replaced them with new yarn. I then glued canvas to the back with latex while it was still on the blocking board. I even glued the binding in place. Finally it was relined.

Corners are nice and square now and maybe I'll get around to putting a new fringe on the edges soon.

172

Bibliography

McHugh, Maureen Collins, *How to Wet Clean Undyed Cotton*, Smithsonian Institution, Wash., D. C.

Method of Cleaning Textiles. Smithsonian Institution, Wash., D. C.

Plenderleith & Werner, *The Conservation of Antiquities and Works of Art.* Oxford University Press, London.

Removing Stains From Fabrics. U. S. Department of Agriculture, Wash., D. C.

Rice, James W., *Principles of Textile Conservation Science.* Textile Museum, Wash., D. C.

Storage of Textiles. Smithsonian Institution, Wash., D. C.

Threads of History. The American Federation of Arts, N. Y., N. Y.

Recommended Products

DESCRIPTION	NAME & SIZE	WHERE TO BUY IT	MANUFACTURER
Acrylic Spray—Use to spray canvas before working to prevent design from running.	Tuffilm Krylon Crystal Clear	Art supply stores Art supply stores	M. Grumbacher, Inc. Borden Chemical Co.
Adhesive Tapes—Use to hold zippers, linings & interlinings in place for stitching.	Double-Sided Adhesive Tape Talon Zipper Adhesive	Fabric stores & Notions counters	Conso Products Co. Talon
Blocking Device—Use to block needlework up to 32″	Meyer Needlepoint Blocking Device	Mail order only	Meyer Enterprises Box 644, Sharon, Pa. 16146
Canvas Plier—Use for stretching needlepoint canvas.	No. 1 Canvas Plier	Art Supply stores	Winsor & Newton, Inc.
Cork—Use for bottom of coasters & trivets. Glue on with latex adhesive.	Self-Stick Cork	Hardware stores	Manton Cork Corp. Merrick, L. I. New York, 11568
Curved Needles—Use for hand stitching.	Clark's Home Craft Asst. Article H–38	Notions departments Fabric stores	Coat's & Clark's
Dacron Batting—Use for large cushions & upholstery.	Fibercoil 76	Upholsterer's supplies	Dupont
Dacon Pillow Forms	Pop-In-Pillow	Needlework shops & Upholstery fabric shops	Fairfield Processing Co. Danbury, Conn. 06810

DESCRIPTION	NAME & SIZE	WHERE TO BUY IT	MANUFACTURER
Drive Punch—Use to make holes in needlework for snaps etc.	Round Drive Punch (5 sizes)	Send for catalog	Tandy Leather Co. 1001 Foch St. Ft. Worth, Texas 76107
Eyelets—Use for holes in belts etc.	AA Eyelets (small) Medium Eyelets (med.)	Send for catalog	Tandy Leather Co. 1001 Foch St. Ft. Worth, Texas, 76107
Fusing Tape	Presto Fusing Tape	Notions departments	Belding–Corticelli
Heat-Proof Glass—Use for trivets.	Pyrex	Consult your local plate glass company.	Corning Glass Co.
Interlinings—Plastic coated fabric used for stiffening.	Perma-Crin (lt. weight) Permette (heavy weight)	Drapery fabric stores	Conso Products Co.
Invisible Thread—Use for hand or machine stitching.	Sew-Gude (lt. weight) Conso HT Monofil #40, Color 1 (heavy weight)	Notions departments Upholsterer's supplies	Gudebrod Bros. Silk Co. Conso Products Co.
Latex Adhesives—Use as fabric cement.	Tri-Tix Rubber Glue (liquid) Tri-Tix Rubber Cream (paste)	Crafts shops Art supply stores	Tri-Tix, Div of Kelch Corp. 6411 W. Mequon Road Mequon, Wisc. 53092
Leather—Use for linings & cushions.	Many types and colors available.	Send for catalog	Tandy Leather Co. 1001 Foch St. Ft. Worth, Texas 76107
Plastic Ruler—Use for measuring.	C-Thru Ruler (18″)	Art supply stores	C-Thru Ruler Co.
Rice Flour—Use for sizing & washable paste.	Byrd Mill Rice Flour	Gourmet food stores Grocery stores	Byrd Mill Co. Richmond, Va. 23220
Shoe Cement—Use for gluing leather to wood etc.	Craftsman Cement	Send for catalog	Tandy Leather Co. 1001 Foch Street Ft. Worth, Texas 76107

DESCRIPTION	NAME & SIZE	WHERE TO BUY IT	MANUFACTURER
Shoe Nails—Use for tacking needlework to wooden soles.	Sole nails (6/8″)	Send for catalog	Tandy Leather Co. Ft. Worth, Texas 76107
Snaps—Use with matching size setter.	Glove snaps (sm.) Belt snaps (med.) Dot Fasteners (lg.)	Send for catalog	Tandy Leather Co. 1001 Foch St. Ft. Worth, Texas 76107
Soil Resistant Sprays—Use last to prevent staining.	Conso Stain Guard Scotch Guard	Fabric stores Upholsterer's supplies	Conso Products Co. 3 M Co.
Stainless Steel Pins—Use for blocking.	"T" Blocking Pins Clinton Wig Pins	Knit Shops Drug stores	The Boye Needle Co. Scovill Mfg. Co.
Steamers—Use for blocking needlework & final pressing.	"Today" Iron Oster Steam Wand Jiffy Steamer, Model 2 (professional, for shops)	Housewares departments Purchase from manufacturer	Sunbeam Corp. John Oster Mfg. Co. Jiffey Steamer Co. Fulton, Ky.
Ultrasuede—Use for linings & pillow backs; washable & dry cleanable.	Comes in many colors 36″ wide.	Dress fabric shops	Skinner Fabrics
Upholsterer's Pins	No. 829, 16 gauge, 3″	Upholsterer's supplies	George W. Mount Greenfield, Mass.
Wooden Soles—Use for sandals. May be painted.	Clogs are available in regular shoe sizes.	Send for catalog	Tandy Leather Co. 1001 Foch St. Ft. Worth, Texas 76107

Needlework Sources

Greengage Designs, P. O. Box 9683, Washington, D. C. 20016:
  checkbook cover, doorstops, fly swatter, handbag, ice bucket, strawberry key holder

The Antique Needle, 8008 Norfolk Ave., Bethesda, Maryland, 20014:
  coat hanger

Woolworks, Inc., 783 Madison Ave., New York, N. Y. 10021:
  floor cushion

The Williams Mfg. Co., West Townsend, Mass., 01474:
  drapery tieback

Joan Toggitt, Ltd., Room 406, 1170 Broadway, New York, N. Y. 10001:
  slippers, wall hanging (both Lindhorst)

Index

Index

B

Bathroom Seat Cover   36
Bell Pull   42
Belts   45
Bias Cording   27
Binding Stitch   31
Blind Stitch   24
Bolster   61

C

Coasters   52
Coat Hangers   54
Color, Bleeding or
   Running   116
Cord, Twisted   33

Cording, Bias   27
Cosmetics Case   105
Covers
     Book   49
     Checkbook   108
Cushions   56

D

Dog Coat   62
Doorstops   64

F

Fly Swatter   67
Footstools   69

G
Glass Cases   73

H
Handbag   112

I
Ice Bucket   75

J
Jewelry Roll   77

K
Key Chains   81

L
London Shrink   19
Luggage Rack Straps   44

M
Mildew   116

N
Needle Case   83

P
Pictures   86
Pincushions   100

R
Rugs   90

S
Sandals   97
Scissors Case   103
Sizing   34
Slippers, Bedroom   38
Stains
        Grease   116
        Rust   117

T
Toe Stuffers   100
Tie-Backs   110
Trivets   52

W
Wall Hangings   101
Waste Basket   115

Credits

PHOTOGRAPHY: Bob Burchette

ILLUSTRATIONS: John Douglass

NEEDLEWORK: Mrs. G. A. Archer—Coat Hanger, Bell Pull.

Miss Lee Hanley—Cosmetic Case, Scissors Case.

Mr. Ferdinand LaMotte, III—Bird & Possum Rugs.

Mrs. E. Sanford—Belts, Footstools, Jewel Roll, Lion Seat Cover, Wall Hanging.

Mrs. Peter Sturtevant & Mrs. Arthur Edgeworth—Checkbook Cover, Door Stops, Fly Swatter, Handbag, Ice Bucket, Strawberry Key Holder.

Sarah Tenenblatt, M.D.—Dog Coat

Miss Avril Thomas—Cushions, Pictures, Slippers, Jonquil Rug.